# Finding the Way

## The Life of a Seeker

## Y. R. LACSKA

*Finding the Way*

Copyright © 2024 Y.R. Lacska
All rights reserved.

No part of this publication may be reproduced, stored in a retrieval system
or transmitted in any way by any means, electronic, mechanical, photocopy,
recording or otherwise without the prior permission of the author except
as provided by USA copyright law.

The opinions expressed by the author are not necessarily those of
Wisdom House Books, Inc.

Published by Wisdom House Books, Inc.
Chapel Hill, North Carolina 27517 USA
www.wisdomhousebooks.com

Wisdom House Books is committed to excellence in the publishing industry.
All rights reserved.

Interior Design by Ted Ruybal
Cover Design by David Spohn
Published in the United States of America

Paperback ISBN: 979-8-218-27011-7
LCCN: 2023920421

1. SEL021000 | SELF-HELP / Motivational / Inspirational
2. REL062000 | RELIGION / Spirituality
3. SOC011000 | SOCIAL SCIENCES / Folklore & Mythology

First Edition

25 24 23 22 21 20 / 10 9 8 7 6 5 4 3 2 1

"Not all who wander are lost!" so said Tolkien's Strider and Y.R. Lacska confirms the wisdom of that counsel. Lacska's book is a spiritual adventure and heroic journey, that invites you to be an adventurer, too. He invites the reader to travel with him on his personal journey and in walking with him, you will discover the Spirit's presence in your own peregrinations. Joining theology, spirituality, and autobiography, this book will inspire your own holistic and heroic adventures. When I opened the book, I couldn't put it down. I saw my own journey in Lacska's journey, and I know you will find a fellow pilgrim in reading this book as well. It will be solved in the walking and Y.R. Lacska is a worthy companion on the way.

—Bruce Epperly

*itheologian, spiritual guide, pastor, and author of numerous books including"The Elephant is Running: Process and Open and Relational Theology and Religious Pluralism."*

There is an important dimension in qigong that is difficult to evaluate by Western science standards. This is the degree of one's ability to move energy. From the standpoint of my own experience, developed under Grandmaster Hong Liu, whose abilities have been documented scientifically at the University of Southern California, Y.R. Lacska displays an aptitude and energy ability of a quite advanced practitioner. Grandmaster Hong also taught him a practice that is only for those of advanced ability. Dr. Lacska also demonstrated his aptitude to me informally, as a consulting peer in clinical psychology offering very helpful suggestions on how to apply qigong in my work with the psychotherapy clients I was seeing at the time.

—Lynn Thomas, PhD

*is a nonprofit organization and management consultant and a qigong and yoga instructor who holds a PhD in clinical psychology.*

In his book, Finding the Way: The Life of a Seeker, Y.R. Lacska offers the reader his Life Story in the presentation of insightful moments which have occurred in his life. Many of his stories seemed totally unconnected, only to be revealed later as inextricably linked. I have known and worked with Reverend Lacska in a partnership of Spiritual Care and Integrative Health Services. He embodied both spiritual ministry and holistic arts expertise. In his book, he reveals the enlightenment that can come from living an examined life. A life of both physical and philosophical wanderings helped him recognize that when the student is ready the teacher will indeed appear. He demonstrates that deep lessons can be excavated from the path that is our life, if one "sits with" all of life's experiences. He weaves together a tapestry of his life experiences, and in so doing, inspires each of us to "sit" with our own life stories with a beginner's mind but also as an open vessel.

—Valerie Lincoln, PHD, RN, AHN-BC

*is an author and leader and in integrative health and holistic nursing practice.*

Y.R. Lacska's Finding the Way: The Life of a Seeker is an extraordinary book that takes the reader on an adventure, a holy pilgrimage through his life and his abundant knowledge of so much—from fairytales, myths, and mystics to Joseph Campbell's hero journey and Carl Jung's knowledge of dreams. Through the stories he values and shares from his own life, he encourages readers to do the same. Lacska writes in a pleasing and felicitous style, with an honest voice and a rich sense of humor, describing joys and pleasures as well as dreams and dark nights. I highly recommend this book.

—Ed Sellner

*is professor emeritus of theology and spirituality at St. Catherine University, St. Paul, Minnesota, and the author of numerous books, his most recent Celtic Saints and Animal Stories: A Spiritual Kinship.*

# Contents

Chapter 1: Not All Who Wander Are Lost . . . . . . . . . . . . . . . . . . . . . . . 1

Chapter 2: The Journey Begins . . . . . . . . . . . . . . . . . . . . . . . . . . . . . . 15

Chapter 3: The Way of Kung Fu . . . . . . . . . . . . . . . . . . . . . . . . . . . . . 33

Chapter 4: The Path of the Counselor . . . . . . . . . . . . . . . . . . . . . . . . 49

Chapter 5: The Dark Night of the Soul . . . . . . . . . . . . . . . . . . . . . . . 59

Chapter 6: Meeting the Goddess . . . . . . . . . . . . . . . . . . . . . . . . . . . . 71

Chapter 7: The Paths Begin to Converge . . . . . . . . . . . . . . . . . . . . . 79

Chapter 8: The Way of the Shen Fu . . . . . . . . . . . . . . . . . . . . . . . . . . 99

Chapter 9: Spirits, Ghosts, and Dreams . . . . . . . . . . . . . . . . . . . . . . 113

Chapter 10: Synchronicity . . . . . . . . . . . . . . . . . . . . . . . . . . . . . . . . 137

Chapter 11: The Three Paths Converge . . . . . . . . . . . . . . . . . . . . . 151

Chapter 12: One Thing . . . . . . . . . . . . . . . . . . . . . . . . . . . . . . . . . . . 167

PostScript . . . . . . . . . . . . . . . . . . . . . . . . . . . . . . . . . . . . . . . . . . . . . . 179

Bibliography . . . . . . . . . . . . . . . . . . . . . . . . . . . . . . . . . . . . . . . . . . . . 183

Acknowledgements . . . . . . . . . . . . . . . . . . . . . . . . . . . . . . . . . . . . . . 191

About the Author . . . . . . . . . . . . . . . . . . . . . . . . . . . . . . . . . . . . . . . 193

# Dedication

*To Wendy*

*With you, my life and this book are complete.*

*To borrow from Emily Bronte*

*Whatever our souls are made of*

*Yours and mine are the same.*

# Chapter One

# *Not All Who Wander are Lost*

So come and walk awhile with me and share
The twisting trails and wondrous worlds I've known.
Shel Silverstein, The Bridge

"Not all who wander are lost." J.R.R. Tolkien penned this famous line in his poem called the "Riddle of Strider," which describes the mysterious character Aragorn in the first book of his *Lord of the Rings* trilogy.

I've always enjoyed wandering. As a child, I loved to roam, exploring the three-acre property of our home in rural Pinellas Park, Florida, and the undeveloped land nearby. Fire trails cut through the sandy thickets of saw palmetto, pine, and live oak trees made it possible to walk through the tangle without getting cut or stabbed by saw palmetto thorns. Just a short way from our house, Joe's Creek flowed wide and deep, the huge trees on its bank replete with what we called "Tarzan vines." My brother Paul, my friends, and I would climb trees so we could use these vines to swing high and out over the creek, letting go at just the right time to fly through the air before splashing into the water.

One of my favorite places was a hollow spot left at the base of a big old fallen tree in the wooded part of our property. I loved to sit in that hollow, observing the vegetation around me and watching the animals and birds, hoping one would come close enough to touch. I would let my imagination create new stories, which I would later act out in play. I loved that old tree hollow…that is, until a large colony of big, menacing-looking brown-and-black ants took possession of my favorite resting place as if daring me to sit there.

This setting afforded a delightful backdrop in which to grow up, letting my youthful imagination run wild in play. I could be Tarzan one day and Robinson Crusoe the next, an explorer from Arthur Conan Doyle's *Lost World* or a spaceman visiting a distant planet. In my early teens, I broadened my wanderings to include new creeks, ponds, and other "secret" places. I even discovered an old, uninhabited Southern mansion near our second home in Madeira Beach and explored its grounds replete with neglected gardens, a large long unused fountain, and moss-covered statuary. Upon discovering an unlocked door, I covertly entered the long-abandoned stately house to find furniture covered with white sheets, cobwebs in the corners and between stair rails, and a great room graced by an out-of-tune grand piano. Remembering this scene now brings to mind Miss Havisham's mansion in Charles Dickens' *Great Expectations* or a foreboding old gothic manor house in one of the Hammer Horror films from the nineteen sixties. I lived in what author Dr. Craig Chalquist calls the "world of childhood magic."

My parents were wanderers too. Both were born in Pennsylvania, my mother Annetta in 1911 and my father Paul in 1913. As a toddler, Mom was moved to Panama, returning to New York to attend nursing college. At age twelve, Dad was moved back to his family's native Hungary; he returned to the U.S. in 1934 to live with a Hungarian family in Long Island, New York. My parents met on a blind date in New York City in the autumn of 1941, where Mom worked as a nurse and Dad served in the Army Air Corps. After their first date, they were inseparable. On the back of a photo, I found of Mom and Dad, taken shortly after they met, was the handwritten comment, "Love at first sight."

When the Japanese bombed Pearl Harbor, Dad asked Mom to marry him, knowing he would probably be deployed because of the war. According to Mom, Dad would sit on her front steps until she agreed to marry him. Then she would always add, "I felt sorry for the poor guy, so I said I would

## Chapter One: Not All Who Wander are Lost

marry him." When we asked Dad if this was true, he would just shrug his shoulders with a little smile on his face.

Mom and Dad's personalities were very different. Dad was quiet and introverted like me, while mom was a talker and an extrovert. They were deeply in love with each other and always treated each other with kindness and respect.

After World War II, my parents moved to Florida, where they finally settled. My only sibling, brother Paul, was born in 1945 before the move. I was born at St. Anthony's Hospital on May 11, 1950. My birth name was John Russell Lacska, but I did not know this until I was forty-four years old. Growing up, I was always called Yanchy (pronounced yahn-chee). It wasn't until I had to present a copy of my birth certificate for a Wisconsin driver's license that I saw the name on my birth certificate was John. I was shocked.

The best reason I have for this surprising discovery is as follows: My immigrant dad called me Yanchy, the Hungarian equivalent of "Johnny," the nickname for "John." My mom apparently liked this and started calling me Yanchy too. After Mom's death, I found my baby book. On the first page she crossed out the name "John"—originally penned in with blue ink which was faded but still somewhat visible—and wrote "Yanchy" over it, not knowing the correct Hungarian spelling was actually "Jancsi." My legal name today is Yanchy Russell Lacska.

My wandering continued when I graduated from high school and meandered from college to college—four in total—including a sophomore year in Luxembourg. I finally graduated with bachelor's and master's degrees from the University of South Florida. I then migrated from Florida to Minnesota, where I took a job helping establish a program for children with autism. I was accepted into the doctoral program in educational psychology at the University of Minnesota. It was there that my three beautiful children, Deborah, Christine, and John, were born adding a new sense of purpose to my life.

Throughout my adult life, I still loved to wander. Today most of my wandering is along trails, through state and national parks or other countries. A favorite rambling memory comes from our last trip to Germany, where we hiked from the town of Moselkern through an ancient forest and along a small river trail to the castle of Burg Eltz. The blue sky peeking through the majestic pines, the sound of the rapidly flowing stream rushing over submerged rocks, and the occasional glimpses of the castle above us allowed me to return to my childhood fantasies. I could imagine myself as Aragorn on his quest.

I always enjoy pausing to rest and just observe everything around me. While my wife Wendy stops to take reference photos for some future oil painting, I hang nearby and simply examine the beauty around me in silent enjoyment: a vista view, a moss-covered rock, or a simple, single flower. The Jewish teacher Yeshua (Jesus) of Nazareth once recommended we, "Consider the wild flowers . . . ," and, "Consider the birds of the air . . . " In the Aramaic language he spoke, the word "consider" translates more accurately to "contemplate or meditate upon," so I suppose these times are a form of meditation on the beauty of nature for me.

On my journey through life, I have tried to follow the Way of Jesus, first through the Roman Catholic tradition. My parents were devout Catholics; Mom was raised in the Roman Catholic tradition and Dad in the Byzantine Catholic tradition. My brother and I attended St. Paul Catholic Elementary School, and I attended Clearwater Central Catholic High School. My first post-high school year was at St. Leo College (now University) in Florida.

My family attended Mass every Sunday, and Catholic nuns and priests were occasional guests at our dinner table. Like other Catholic families in the 1950s and 60s, we abstained from eating meat on Fridays, and during

Lent we prayed the rosary as a family every Friday evening—my brother, mother, and I kneeling on the floor while my dad sat on the couch, which didn't seem very fair to me.

As an elementary school student at St. Paul's, I would often go into the church during recess, just long enough to dip my fingers in the holy water font, make the sign of the cross, and say a couple of quick prayers to gain a little more grace. To my young mind, communicating with God was like using a spiritual telephone. You could only reach God or Jesus or Mary by dialing in the correct phone number via the prayers that were taught at school and at home. In my childish view, Catholicism was a sort of religious cultural club in which my family and friends were privileged to be members. Catholic doctrines, as taught by the Franciscan sisters, were truths to be believed and rules to be obeyed. And, of course, I was taught that the Roman Catholic Church was the one true church.

The older I got, the more I adapted society's conventions that dismissed the world of enchantment in which I loved to play as a boy. But even though I began questioning the reality of the unseen world, I continued to hang on to the metaphysical beliefs of the Catholic Church, attending Sunday Mass until my thirties. However, it seemed the more I read about philosophy, spirituality, and religion, the farther I grew away theologically from Roman Catholic teachings. My split from the Church became final when I was no longer welcome to participate in Holy Communion after divorcing and remarrying. Communion had always been, and still is, an important part of my religious life.

The earliest followers of Rabbi Yeshua (Jesus) called themselves the Followers of the Way. The more my hair turned gray at the temples, the more it seemed to me that "the Way" of Jesus was meant to be a journey, a lived experience rather than a set of doctrines. I came to agree with Pelagius—considered a saint by some and a heretic by others—who taught that church doctrines were inventions of the human mind in its attempt to understand the mystery of God. Author and minister Brian McLaren reinforced my thinking when I read his book *We Make the Road by Walking*. He argued that the Christian faith was intended to be a way of living, one that remains creative and unfinished while still appreciating what has been learned from the past.

For me, there are two paths for walking the Way of Jesus. The first is through the Jewish and Christian scriptures . . . provided we understand the stories as mythic accounts written to express the writers' understanding of the mystery we call God in a certain time and place in history. The second path, as taught by the Celtic Christians, is through the natural world. Saint Bernard of Clairvaux expressed this when he wrote in *On Loving God*, "What I know of the divine sciences and the Holy Scriptures, I have learned in woods and fields. I have no other masters than the beaches and the oaks." American transcendentalist philosopher Ralph Waldo Emerson also understood this, as evidenced by his lecture comment, "Nature is too thin a screen; the glory of the omnipresent God bursts through everywhere."

For me, finding the Divine in nature has become an important means of seeking and following the Way, and I have learned a great deal from the writings of the transcendentalists, the Celtic Christians, and the Taoists.

To celebrate our fourth wedding anniversary, Wendy and I drove to the North Shore of Lake Superior and stayed for a week at Solbakken Resort, our favorite "Up North" retreat, in rustic Cabin Four. Built in the 1930s, Cabin Four was perched on a ledge just above the rock shore of Lake Superior, and the same small two-bedroom cabin in which Wendy and I nestled for sixteen days on our honeymoon.

## Chapter One: Not All Who Wander are Lost

Framed drawings depicting local scenes hung on its cedar walls, blue-and-white checkered cafe curtains hung on the windows. An old-time kitchen filled one side of the room, complete with cabinets made from the same knotty cedar as the walls, porcelain sink, gas range, and a refrigerator similar to the one my family had in the 1950s. Opposite the kitchen was a blue and gray fabric-covered couch and a small bathroom with a toilet, sink, and shower I could barely fit into. In the center of the room, against a window looking out at the old cedar deck on which moss grew encouraged by the moisture from the big lake, was a small dining table on which we always placed a vase of wildflowers. We used one of the two tiny bedrooms to store clothes and other vacation trappings, the other to sleep. A small chest of drawers sat only about a foot away from the double bed which filled the rest of the room, leaving barely enough room to maneuver. The handmade quilt on the bed featured a dark blue underside. We called it the "starry night quilt."

Cabin Four was very special to us. We spent many summer vacations (and a couple of winter ones) in that little cabin until 2011, when it sadly burned down. Although the Solbakken owners built a new Cabin Four in its footprint, it just didn't have the same feeling and memories for us. We stayed in it once, but the new cabin lost the old-time charm, and Wendy cried when we entered the newly built place.

Now, we didn't have anything to do with the burning down of Cabin Four, although we nearly burned it down on our wedding night—and I mean that quite literally. We were married on a warm July day in 1991 at the Lutsen Lodge on the shore of Lake Superior, not far from Solbakken Resort and just beyond the old, covered wooden bridge straddling the Poplar River. After a splendid wedding reception dinner with family and a few good friends at the Lodge's restaurant, we drove to Cabin Four looking forward to a romantic wedding night. Wendy put on the long, white, lacy negligee and slippers she purchased for this special night, and I put on the new robe she bought for me. After placing a variety of candles around the cabin, we began dancing slowly to a CD of our favorite love songs. A cool breeze drifted through the windows, gently moving the curtains. It was a romantic and sensual scene . . . that is, until the wind blew one of the curtains, which had probably been hanging there for fifty years, into the flame of a candle. The curtain burst into flame. Wendy reacted quickly, ripping it off the curtain rod and throwing it onto the floor. I grabbed a big pot of water from the stove (only there because, providentially, a water pipe had broken at the resort and there was no running water) and dumped it on the curtain's flaming blue-and-white checks. Wendy then used her fancy new white slippers to stomp out the flames. So, you see, we actually did set the place on fire on our wedding night.

Back to the morning of our fourth anniversary, we woke up to the sound of the big lake's waves breaking on the rocky shore and the high-pitched call of gulls. Wendy cooked her famous (so she told me) blueberry wild rice pancakes and bacon for breakfast while I made coffee. After leisurely eating our breakfast and enjoying a second cup of coffee, we washed the dishes together before organizing ourselves for a hike. We had purchased the *Guide to the Superior Hiking Trail* at the Trading Post in Grand Marais the previous day, and after looking through it decided to hike the "Moose Mountain to Mystery Mountain" portion of the trail. Our adventure began at the Lutsen Mountain Resort, where we rode the gondola one thousand feet up to the Summit Chalet restaurant on top of Moose Mountain. From there, our book indicated we were to follow a half-mile spur trail to the point where it tied into the Superior Hiking Trail.

We set off on the little spur trail, which offered a beautiful start with its mossy boulders, exposed roots, and a ridge-top view of Moose Mountain to our left. After a short time, we were abruptly confronted by a large, smooth rock which dropped vertically about five feet. We examined the map and it seemed to show the trail continuing straight ahead. We saw

## Chapter One: Not All Who Wander Are Lost

footprints below the rock, indicating others had gone this way. Looking around, we also noticed a series of rough, rudimentary log-and-rock steps switching steeply back uphill. As we deliberated a couple of hikers appeared on the ridge where the steps led. We asked them if the trail continued that way, but they said that after traveling it, the trail appeared to end at a fallen tree.

So, we decided to continue climbing down the rock and walking along what soon became a very narrow ledge of mud, rocks, and roots with a shear rock wall rising up on our left and a drop-off through the woods to our right. My intuition, or perhaps my fear, told me that this could *not* be the designated trail. But my intellectual and logical brain kept saying, "What about the map? What about the other hikers?" As we continued along the ledge, I couldn't help thinking about the scenes in the Saturday matinee movies of my childhood where the characters would cautiously shuffle along a ledge until someone inevitably fell off into the hot lava below. While there was no hot lava at the bottom of Moose Mountain, a fall would have certainly caused serious injury if it didn't kill us.

We struggled gingerly along the precarious path for what seemed be an hour until we came to a cleared steep slope that seemed like it must be a ski run during the winter. Now, knowing this couldn't be the trail we were supposed to be hiking, we debated whether we should try to climb up to the top of this slope or slide down the slope on our bottoms using our feet as brakes, hoping to see some kind of road or path through the woods from there. While we talked about what option was best, we saw two people at the top of the slope. Wendy called out and asked them if they knew the location of the Superior Hiking Trail. They said, "Yes, we are on it!" We clambered up the (maybe) hundred feet to the top of the steep slope and found the trail above us.

It was now just after three o'clock in the afternoon, and we had dinner reservations at the Lutsen Lodge Restaurant for five-thirty. Wendy really wanted to finish the hike but I was afraid we would miss our anniversary dinner time and lose the special table where we had sat the night of our wedding reception dinner...not to mention being too tired for any intimacy on our anniversary night!

The hiking book indicated that it was a three-hour hike back to the parking lot. After some discussion, we decided to see where the Superior Hiking Trail began to descend Moose Mountain, then backtrack to the gondola down to the parking lot. When we arrived at the point where a sign indicated a connection the Moose Mountain/Mystery Mountain portion of the trail, we saw a woman and man sitting and relaxing. the man lounging between the exposed roots of a large maple to lean against its tree trunk and the woman sitting on a large boulder. The scene brought to my mind fairy tales in which the characters come to a fork in the path and an old woman or man, a gnome, or a speaking animal is there to help, provided they are treated respectfully and their advice is heeded by the traveler. The couple told us that they had just hiked up along that same route we had planned, and that it only took them two hours, with a couple ten-minute breaks on the way up.

Again, my mind thought, "But the book says three hours." I found myself struggling internally between following the advice of the helpful strangers or following the logical course of action presented by my ego. The couple offered another piece of advice: "If it doesn't look like the trail, it's not." This advice would have certainly been helpful had we known and heeded it earlier.

Even though Wendy wanted to continue the hike, she said it was okay to return via the gondola. However, not wanting to disappoint her and also curious, said, "Let's go for it." So, we bid goodbye to the couple and headed down the Lake Superior Hiking Trail. The path took us down Moose Mountain and up and down Mystery Mountain; well worth it. There were some very lovely scenic overlooks and as we traveled down in elevation the forest changed from cedar and pine to mostly maple and—finally—to birch and poplar, giving us a variety of visual treats. This portion of the trail ended upon crossing the Poplar River at the scenic Lower Falls. From there, it was a short walk to the parking lot and our car. We felt very proud to have finished the hike, and we did it in exactly two hours, just as the friendly couple said. We stopped at the Lutsen Lodge Restaurant and changed our dinner reservation for later in the evening, so it all worked out very well.

Our adventure on Mouse and Mystery Mountains reminds me of the Tolkien verse with which I began this chapter, that not all who wander are lost. In fact, I suspect that many who are wandering around—seemingly lost, even to themselves—are really not lost at all in the sense that their wanderings are meaningless or without purpose. Myths and fairy tales tell us this over and over again. The Round Table knight Percival wanders for five years trying to find the Holy Grail. The Greek hero Odysseus wanders for ten years before he returns to his home in Ithaca after the Trojan war. In the Chinese story *Journey to the West*, the Buddhist monk Xuánzàng, goes on a sixteen-year pilgrimage to obtain sacred Buddhist religious texts. In each of these stories, the wanderer gains moral and spiritual insights which tell us that wandering has a purpose.

The naturalist and philosopher John Muir didn't like the term "hiking." He preferred people "saunter" through the wilderness. He pointed out that the term "saunter" originated in the Middle Ages and referred to people on a pilgrimage from France to the Holy Land. When people met these pilgrims and asked where they were going, their reply was, *a' la sainte terre*, to the Holy Land. Over time, these pilgrims became known as "saunterers."

As we wander through life, we are all saunterers. We usually think that the goal of a pilgrimage is to reach some holy or spiritually significant physical destination, and Wendy and I have included this type of pilgrimage in our travels. We have sauntered to Chartres Cathedral to walk the labyrinth, to the island of Iona, to the Chalice Well in Glastonbury, to Uluru at the center of Australia, and to other sacred places. But over the course of my life, I have come to see *every* place as holy. The more important pilgrimage is the internal one that the Eastern Christian Church calls "theosis" or Carl Jung called "individuation."

This idea is expressed in song during the evening Celtic Contemplative Communion service at Pilgrim Lutheran Church in St. Paul. We sing *Peregrination Pro Amore Christi*, proclaiming we are on a pilgrimage for the love of Christ. "Peregrination" is a journey that doesn't proceed along any defined route or lead to a specific destination. It is sauntering or wandering, but not aimlessly. Perhaps this is one way to understand what Jesus was referring to when he said, "You know well enough how the wind blows this way and that. You hear it rustling through the trees, but you have no idea where it comes from or where it's headed next. That's the way it is with everyone born from above by the wind of God, the Spirit of God" (John 3:8 The Message). Perhaps the journey itself is what is important.

In the forward to Viktor Frankl's book *Man's Search for Meaning* Harold S. Kushner wrote, "Life is not primarily a quest for pleasure, as Freud believed, or a quest for power, as Alfred Adler taught, but a quest for meaning. The greatest task for any person is to find meaning in his or her own life." We are all wandering to get know ourselves better, to understand our purpose in the world, to respond to an inner calling that we cannot fully describe or understand, and perhaps to find the enchantment that we lost. We are all on what mythologist Joseph Campbell called the "hero's journey," or what psychologist and mythologist Craig Chalquist terms the "Journey of Re-Enchantment. We are all on a quest to find our personal holy grail, our treasure buried in a field, our philosopher's stone.

Like the heroines, heroes, and wanderers in myth and stories, we don't know how our future will unfold but we can learn to trust our hearts, the helpers along the way, and guidance from the transpersonal. As wanderers, we travel to new places, experience new people, and hopefully come to know ourselves and the Great Mystery at a deeper, more intimate level.

It is not always a journey of comfort. It can be full of challenges and suffering, and it can seem like we are wandering meaninglessly and are lost. But it can also be a journey of learning, beauty, joy, and awe. As Thoreau wrote in *Walden*, "Not till we are lost…not till we have lost the world, do we begin to find ourselves, and realize where we are and the infinite extent of our relations."

## Chapter Two

# *The Journey Begins*

*The path to our destination is not always a straight one.
We go down the wrong road, we get lost, we turn back.
Maybe it doesn't matter which road we embark on.
Maybe what matters is that we embark.*
Barbara Hall, *Northern Exposure* episode "Rosebud," 1993

Reflecting upon my youth and young adulthood, I identify with the sentiment of Swiss psychiatrist Carl Jung when he wrote, "I did not know that I was living a myth, and even if I had known it, I would not have known what sort of myth was ordering my life without my knowledge. So, in the most natural way, I took it upon myself to get to know 'my' myth, and I regarded this as the task of tasks." (Carl Jung, CW 5, Volume 5, pages xxiv-xxv).

That is the foundation of this book. The stories I tell are reflections on how I came to know my own myth and any wisdom that life, this "task of tasks," has afforded me. I now happily pass that wisdom on to you. I became interested in mythology early in my life. In elementary school, I was introduced to *Collier's Junior Classics* and was spellbound by the myths and legends, stories of magic, and hero tales chronicled in these volumes. These entrancing stories led me to read books that were unusual for kids my age. In eighth grade, I remember reading *The Histories* by Herodotus, in which the author facilely mixed history and mythology, and *Bulfinch's Mythology: Stories of Gods and Heroes*. In high school, I read *The Golden Bough: A Study in Magic and Religion* by James George Frazer, even though it was not assigned reading for any class. Before I go on with my story, I want to clarify how I define the term "myth." Myth is a word that is generally thought of by most folks as a story that is untrue or fictitious, often hearing people say, "That's just a myth." When I use the word "myth" I mean a story that conveys some important truth or moral, whether *factually* true or not. Mythic stories always serve some type of societal, psychological, cosmological, or spiritual purpose. Catholic priest and mystic Bede Griffiths once said that all religious stories are myths…symbolic expressions of truths that cannot be fully expressed in any other way. J.R.R. Tolkien said that myths are largely made of truth, often presenting aspects of truth which can only be understood through a mythic story.

Because of this, I no longer ask myself (or a counseling client), "Did this really happen?" or, "Is this how it really happened?" Rather, I ask myself what truth can be found in the story being told that can help this person, or me, find meaning.

Our personal myth shows us how we connect to our society, to intimate others, to ourselves, and to the transpersonal or spiritual. Jung wrote, "Myth is the revelation of a divine life in man." (Jung, *Memories, Dreams, Reflections*) As a counselor who has been strongly influenced by the theories of Jung, I also look at the images within stories, myths, and dreams as universal archetypes.

Archetypes are patterns or symbols that have universal, mythic meaning beyond the natural meaning, often occurring across multiple cultures and throughout time. For example, we all know the archetype of the "good mother" as nurturing, comforting, protective, and loving—"Mother Earth" being the universal archetype embodying these characteristics. The opposite of this is the "bad mother" archetype, often seen in fairytales as a wicked stepmother. Another archetype we undoubtedly encounter on our journey is that of evil, often depicted in story as a monster, the devil, or a villain without conscience—Dracula, or Voldemort from the *Harry Potter* stories being classic examples. Archetypes can also appear as elemental images or objects: water, fire, a mountain, a cave, the sun or moon, or even an everyday item like an automobile.

Jung theorized that archetypes are part of the collective unconscious which contains hereditary ancestral memories. As symbols and psychic agents, translating these archetypes can help us move toward understanding everything from daily challenges to discovering our life's purpose or meaning. On the hero's journey we encounter mythical elements and archetypes, often in our dreams.

Emphasizing this idea, Campbell suggested that every myth and fairy tale follows similar stages of the hero's journey in some manner. Therefore, there is essentially only one myth, which Campbell called the "monomyth." While we can easily recognize the hero's journey of archetypal characters in popular cinema and stories like Luke Skywalker or Rey in *Star Wars*, Neo in the *Matrix*, or Hua Mulan in Disney's *Mulan*, it is not as easy to recognize it in the lives of real people we know, and even more difficult to recognize it in our own life. Most of us are not trained in Chinese martial arts like Mulan and Neo, nor in the ways of the Force like Luke and Rey.

And not all heroes are warriors. Ordinary people also end up on the hero's journey, like fictional characters Dorothy in *The Wizard of Oz* or Phileas Fogg in Jules Verne's *Around the World in 80 Days*. Then there are real-life heroes like Desmond T. Doss, the army medic who in the World War II battle of Okinawa refused to kill or even carry a weapon. He was awarded the Medal of Honor and Bronze Star for his heroism in rescuing seventy-five wounded soldiers in the heat of battle.

Some may object to the use of the term "hero's journey" because "hero" has become a masculine term, and this is understandable. However, in Greek mythology "Hero" was a priestess of Aphrodite who sacrificed her own life to save the life of her lover. The word "hero" is derived from the

Greek word meaning "protector," and probably became a predominantly male term because it evolved in patriarchal societies. For those who, for whatever reason, have difficulty relating to Campbell's hero's journey, professor and author Dr. Craig Chalquist developed what he describes as the "Journey of Re-enchantment," an idea that may make more sense or be more comfortable for some folks. I primarily use Campbell's stages of the hero's journey as the framework of my story. But when they seem to illuminate an idea more fully or provide a new perspective to my narrative, I also include the ideas Chalquist expressed in his *HuffPost* blog "Why I Seldom Teach The Hero's Journey Anymore—And What I Teach Instead."

As I mentioned earlier, I have come to think we will *all* find ourselves on the hero's journey during our lives. In his discussions with reporter Bill Moyers in the PBS television series *The Power of Myth*, Joseph Campbell clarified that the hero's journey isn't limited to mythological archetypes, stories, and fairy tales. Far from it. This mythic journey applies to each and every one of us. While our individual lives entail distinctive storylines, they all seem to adhere to this singular archetypal structure, lived out by women and men from all times and in every culture.

Unlike most stories in novels and films, our personal hero's journey—our myth, our "task of tasks"—is not a one-time adventure, but rather a cycle of themes that can regenerate in various manifestations throughout our lives. In my life the hero's journey has taken three distinct roads, each of which emerged and rematerialized at various times in my life, sometimes intersecting. These journeys eventually converged onto one path. This conversion, allowed me to write my doctoral dissertation which put forward and validated the benefits of an integrated approach to transpersonal counseling.

According to Joseph Campbell, the hero's journey begins in the "ordinary world" of everyday life. The hero is often innocent and naive, sometimes

## Chapter Two: The Journey Begins

living in the world of enchantment that Craig Chalquist refers to in his *HuffPost* article as the "Islands and Oases of Childhood Magic," where there is a thin divide between the logical world of adults, make-believe, dreams, and daydreams. Sometimes the story's hero is bored and fantasizes about a more adventurous life, like Dorothy, who lived with her Auntie Em and Uncle Henry on their Kansas farm, wondering about life "somewhere over the rainbow." Or Luke Skywalker, living with his uncle and aunt on the desert planet Tatooine and longing to be a pilot. Other would-be heroes are quite comfortable with their uneventful life, like Bilbo Baggins in Tolkien's *The Hobbit* and young Jim Hawkins in Robert Louis Stevenson's novel, *Treasure Island*.

The mythic journey always begins with some kind of a Call to Adventure. This call is usually heralded by some type of triggering event that causes a disruption of ordinary life. Dorothy's little dog Toto is taken away by Miss Gulch. When Toto escapes from Miss Gulch and returns, Dorothy runs away to save her beloved pet. In *Star Wars*, Luke has to search for a runaway droid and meets Obi Wan Kenobi. Bilbo's call to adventure begins when thirteen unexpected and uninvited dwarves pay him a visit. Jim Hawkins' call to adventure begins with a pirate encounter and the discovery of a treasure map.

My first Call to Adventure came when I was in fourth grade, living the ordinary life of a nine-year-old in the ordinary world of school and home. During school one day, I developed a stomach ache that became increasingly painful as the day progressed. By the afternoon I couldn't concentrate anymore, so I put my head down on my desk and held my stomach. My teacher asked what was wrong and, after the pain didn't go away, walked me to the office where the secretary telephoned my mother. After arriving home, Mom made me a traditional home remedy tea for stomachache. I drank the tea, and she placed a hot water bottle on my stomach and covered me with a blanket. Day turned into evening and Dad came home from work, but the pain in my stomach intensified. I developed a fever. My parents decided it was time to telephone our local family doctor. After asking Mom a few questions, the doctor told us to meet him at the hospital; it sounded like I had appendicitis.

As soon as we arrived at the small Sun Coast Hospital, I was evaluated and quickly prepped for an emergency appendectomy. Nervous and embarrassed, I kept my eyes closed as a nurse washed and shaved my lower abdomen (strange, since I didn't have any hair there yet). My anxiety increased as I was wheeled down the hallway and pushed through the foreboding metal double doors into the operating room. Seeing the bright lights and doctors and nurses in their masks and gowns was even more distressful. A kind nurse anesthetist talked calmly while putting a black mask over my face, which, she pointed out, was like the one worn by a jet fighter pilot. She told me to count backwards from ten to one; I counted a couple of numbers before everything went black.

Then, while the surgical team worked desperately to save my life, I had a near-death experience or NDE.

I found myself floating above the operating room, watching the doctors and nurses working on my body below. I wasn't frightened anymore, only confused. Then I experienced what can best be described as flying in hyperspace through some kind of tunnel of light.

The next thing I knew was I was standing in a beautiful grassy field amid a variety of colorful flowers. I felt completely at peace. Several people, who I did not recognize, were walking toward me and smiling. Then I saw a man that I somehow knew immediately was Jesus. He walked up to me, put his hands on my shoulders, and, looking into my eyes, smiled and said everything would be okay. I don't remember everything he said, but the last thing was, "You have to go back because your mommy and daddy will miss you too much if you stay." Then he hugged me.

## Chapter Two: The Journey Begins

The next thing I remember was waking up in my hospital room and telling mom and dad not to worry because I had seen Jesus and he told everything would be all right. During my recovery at the hospital, I was visited by Father John McCall, a local priest. I overheard Mom tell him that my appendix had ruptured and that the surgeon said they almost lost me on the operating table. Being a devout Catholic, Mom was also sure to tell him I had seen Jesus. She believed this experience was a sign from God that I was called to be a priest. Father McCall gave me a wooden crucifix surrounded by white, plastic, glow-in-the dark stations of the cross. I have always cherished his gift, which still hangs on the wall above my office desk at home.

After recovering from my appendectomy, life quickly returned to normal and I soon forgot about my NDE, or at least stored the experience somewhere in the back of my mind. I certainly didn't realize how this experience impacted my life until many years later when I attended a psychology conference and heard an expert panel discussing NDE experiences. The more I listened, the more astonished I was by how much I had in common with other adults who had a near-death experience as a child.

Children who experienced a NDE have increased empathy and sensitivity to the emotions of others and are much more likely to end up working in a helping profession. Long before I became a psychologist or a minister, people naturally came to me with their problems. Wendy says this is because "I see people." Like most other NDE folks, I become sad or angry when I hear about or see violence or maltreatment toward people or animals. I find it distressing to hear violent news reports, watch graphic violence in movies, or read violent accounts in books. Also common to NDE kin is being uncomfortable in crowds. I never enjoy large concerts, the State Fair, or large parties.

Another shared characteristic is my fervent interest in spirituality and mystery. As mentioned above, I developed a hunger for mythology at a young age. This interest grew and broadened over the years and books on myth, spirituality and religion continue to be a mainstay of my reading preferences.

Lastly, like other NDE folks, I do not fear death. It's not that I look forward to death or desire it in any way. To the contrary, I want to stay alive here on earth with Wendy and family and friends as long as possible. I want to live my life to the fullest. But the thought of dying doesn't scare or worry me. Because of my near-death experience, when someone asks me whether I believe in life after death, my response is always, "I don't believe. I know."

Even though my life after my NDE was firmly grounded in the ordinary world, the enchanted or mystical world was always lurking in the background and would occasionally break through. When I was in seventh grade, I became an altar boy at Sacred Heart Parish near our home. While serving at Mass one morning, I had a mystical—or what Carl Jung would call numinous—experience. As the priest elevated the consecrated host above his head, I felt a charge of powerful and pleasurable energy run from him, down my arm, and through my entire body. The feeling left me in a reverie for the rest of the Mass.

Being a good Catholic boy, and likely influenced by my mom and Fr. McCall's crucifix gift, I accepted the idea that I was called to become a priest. Our pastor arranged for me to attend the same pre-seminary high school he had attended. However, adolescence arrived in full bloom the summer after eighth grade along with my first adolescent crush and the kissing, intimate touching, and the surging sex hormones that accompanied it. All of a sudden, the idea of a life of celibacy without ever able to ever act on these feelings became unappealing. So, I decided not to go to pre-seminary and instead attended Clearwater Central Catholic High School.

## Chapter Two: The Journey Begins

I'm sure my mother was disappointed, though she never said so. My father said that I could always go to seminary when I was older if I still felt I had a vocation to the priesthood. Little did I know at the time that I would go to seminary and become ordained as an Orthodox Catholic priest forty-two years later. But we'll get to that story later. Even though I still had a slender thread of connection to the magical and spiritual world of my childhood, I became more and more firmly entrenched in what Chalquist calls the stage of "Disenchantment, Forgetfulness, and Adaptation."

High school life planted me even more firmly in the ordinary world: sports, dating, acting in the school play, and even playing electric bass in a rock-and-roll band called The Rubber Band. Father McCall entered my life again, this time as the principal of Clearwater Central Catholic and religion teacher for the upper classes. Father McCall was the first person to teach religion from a more adult theological perspective, the first to introduce us to other Christian denominations and world religions. During my high school years, major changes also came to the Catholic Church. The priest now faced the congregation instead of facing away and toward the altar or *ad orientem* (to the east), and Latin—the language or ritual and magic—was replaced with English.

These changes created a more "adult" understanding of religion which drove me deeper into what Chalquist calls "Alienation from the Magical" or adaptation to the adult world. In my first two years of college, I wandered from class to class at four different colleges with no real career goal in mind, only wanting to graduate. College courses in philosophy and psychology entrenched me even more deeply into Disenchantment and Alienation from the numinous world.

The first college I attended was Saint Leo in Florida. It was the first time I lived away from home, and freshman males had to live a dormitory that was part of the Benedictine monastery where we could be supervised and supported by one of the Benedictine brothers. My two roommates and I devised a clever scheme to hide cold beer in our room on the weekend. We put ice and beer in the bottom of one of our cylindrical gray metal waste cans, then cut a round piece of cardboard to place on top, a few inches down from the rim, with wadded up paper glued on to appear normal. Unfortunately, our floor supervisor, Brother Donald, accidentally bumped into the can on a visit to our room and noticed an unusual sloshing sound. Upon further inspection, he discovered our stash of cold beer. Instead of reporting us to the dean, he offered an alternative: He would confiscate the beer and give us a punishment he would devise instead. We accepted his offer, rather than risk more serious consequences from the dean and—worst of all—having our misdeed reported to our parents.

Brother Donald decided we would get up and join the monks for morning prayer for an entire week. Morning prayer was at six o'clock and, while I hated getting up and dressed that early, I actually enjoyed hearing the brothers singing their Gregorian chants. By the end of the week, I was joining in, humming along as best I could. However, I didn't like it enough to continue once my time serving was completed. In addition to this early prayer time, we had to spend the next Saturday cleaning the stables and barn—a very hot, smelly, and overall unpleasant job.

I was lucky to spend my sophomore year as an exchange student through St. Leo at the Vita International Study Center in Luxembourg, housed at the Château d'Ansembourg. I lived with several other young men in a room at the Marienthal Monastery just down the road from the chateau. There, I would sometimes rise early so I could join the Cistercian brothers at morning Mass. While finding comfort in the familiar ritual of Mass, I was *really* more attracted to joining the brothers for their delicious breakfast of croissants, meats, cheeses, fruit, and pastries afterward.

## Chapter Two: The Journey Begins

Being apart from the enchanted world for so long, I almost forget it was there at all. Then one cool and crisp autumn afternoon I took a walk up the wooded hill behind the college when classes were finished for the day, and laid down on the ground, looking skyward through the tall pine trees. There was just enough moisture in the crisp fall air that the subsiding sun created a prismatic effect, filling the air with tiny, sparkling diamonds. I suddenly had a momentary, emotionally charged sensory experience of unity with all creation and of the Divine energies in everything. It only lasted for a few minutes, but it was a wondrous epiphany that the reality of our daily lives is eminently more mysterious than we are aware.

This numinous experience was a lifeline returning me to the enchanted world of holiness and magic. The medieval text, *Cloud of Unknowing*, describes such occurrences as a "state of grace and unity" in which a person experiences the innermost heart of their being and, for the briefest moment, has the realization of being a participant in divine nature.

After returning to college in the United States I decided not to return to Saint Leo, instead wandering again and going first to Southern Illinois University and then to the University of South Florida. While at SIU, I decided to become a special education teacher after visiting a program serving children with various intellectual and physical disabilities as an assignment for a psychology class. Teaching sounded like the perfect profession: I would get paid for being with these amiable kids and have a worthy job helping children. As a bonus, teachers got the summer off. In my mind it couldn't get any better than that.

In reflecting on this now, the words of Luke Skywalker to Rey after she explains her understanding of the Force in *The Last Jedi* seem to apply: "Amazing! Every word of what you just said was wrong." I began my first teaching job as a special education teacher. I quickly discovered that my students, besides being mildly developmentally disabled, were also diagnosed with a variety of mental health and/or behavior disorders for which I was woefully ill prepared to handle. I married right after graduation to my first wife, who also taught at a local Catholic school, and also discovered that being on a teacher's salary meant having to work another job—part-time on weekends and full-time during the summer—just to pay bills.

My planned path, while having these surprises and unexpected turns, still seemed pretty straightforward, with only minor adjustments required. I enrolled in a master's degree program at the University of South Florida which emphasized working with children struggling with mental health and behavioral issues. My new plan was to complete my MA then complete my doctorate in educational psychology, which would give me a decent salary, a high level of professional status, and a future job as either a special education administrator or a college professor.

Everything moved along smoothly, just as I planned. I earned my master's degree and was accepted into the doctoral program in educational psychology at the University of Minnesota. In addition, the St. Paul Public School system hired me to establish a special education program for children with autism. My wandering now took me to the Twin Cities area of Minnesota. After only one course in educational administration, I switched my program emphasis to mental health counseling after realizing I could not be happy as an administrator. This seemed like a fairly minor adjustment on my envisioned path to success in the world, with a new plan to become a licensed psychologist and, eventually, a college professor.

But when we are separated too long from the numinous, it has a way of luring us back. An event occurred which called me to a new hero's journey and set me on a new phase of wandering. Maybe "not all those who wander are lost," but I certainly felt confused and lost for some time on this phase of my journey. When my second-born daughter Christine (Chrissie) was a toddler, she became very ill with a bug, which resulted in a rapidly climbing temperature triggering a febrile seizure. This was a very frightening experience for us as young parents. We bundled her up and took her to the pediatrician, who after examining her, assured us that while this was not dangerous, we should carefully monitor her for another seizure. Late evening, after a long day of worry, I quietly went into the bedroom to check on her. While her older sister, Debi, was asleep in the twin bed on the opposite wall of their small bedroom, Chrissie was in a troubled sleep, her face flushed and hot.

I was tired from the stress and worry of the ordeal, but too charged with emotion to try to sleep. Deeper than any worry or anxiety, however, was the love and compassion I felt for my sick little girl. I sat down slowly and carefully on the edge of Chrissie's bed, trying not to wake her, and placed a cool washcloth on her hot forehead. I was gently and lovingly stroking her blond hair when something happened—something unanticipated and mysterious. As I stroked her hair, a sensation of warmth formed in my chest. Another strong, tangible sensation like a tingling or flow of warm water began to move down my arm, into my hand, and into Chrissie's head. As this happened, her fever broke and she began to sweat. Her skin started cooling rapidly, her breathing slowing and deepening until she fell into a deep and comfortable sleep.

I felt an immense sense of relief and happiness. But I was also bewildered by what had just happened. This became the triggering event which started me on a new quest . . . a quest to discover how this healing "anomaly" had occurred.

My exploration took on both academic and personal dimensions. I read several books on healing, including *The Healing Light* by Agnes Sanford; *Psychology, Religion and Healing* by nonconformist Methodist minister and psychologist Leslie D. Weatherhead; *Healing and Wholeness* by

Episcopalian priest and Jungian analyst John A. Sanford; and *Healing: A Doctor in Search of a Miracle* by Minnesota surgeon and medical advice columnist William A. Nolen. While my reading validated that healing that could not be explained by medical science did indeed occur, there was no agreed-upon convincing explanation as to how these healings occurred nor how to replicate them

At the same time, I sought out groups who maintained a belief in spiritual healing. I contacted the pastor of a local Assemblies of God church who graciously agreed to meet with me over lunch. He explained the Pentecostal church's beliefs regarding healing through the Holy Spirit. It just so happened that I arrived with a swollen and painful sprained ankle from playing basketball with friends. The pastor invited me to his church for a healing prayer session so I could experience spiritual healing personally for my ankle. A few days later, I arrived at his church and was met by the pastor, who ushered me into a room where a small group of maybe five or six people were present. After introductions I was asked to sit in a metal folding chair while the group sat or stood around me.

The pastor began with an opening prayer, and then those praying for me gently touched my ankle, knee, and shoulders while praying for healing. Some prayed in tongues, which was a foreign and somewhat uncomfortable experience for someone like me, raised in the Roman Catholic tradition. When they finished, my ankle still hurt and was just as swollen as when we began. When I pointed this out, I was told that I wasn't healed because I did not have enough faith. Now this seemed very strange to me, since my experience with Chrissie involved neither religious faith nor prayer of any kind. This idea—that one is not healed if they lack faith—has become one of my pet peeves. In fact, it angers me to hear people blame the victim; implying it is somehow their fault if they aren't healed.

## Chapter Two: The Journey Begins

Not long after my experience at the Pentecostal church, a friend was diagnosed with cancer. She was pregnant at the time and declined chemotherapy because she didn't want the treatment to harm the developing fetus. By the time she gave birth to a healthy boy baby, the cancer had metastasized and spread through her body. She and her husband were active in a church that also expressed a belief in spiritual healing. And again, I witnessed people there who told my friend that if she just had enough faith, God would heal her. I felt deep anger toward them, and deep compassion toward her and her family. I visited her regularly, often sitting with her, talking and reading to her while placing cool washcloths on her forehead just as I had with Chrissie a couple of years earlier. But this time no magic happened. She died from her cancer.

I still had no idea what happened with Chrissie, nor how to elicit this healing energy to help others. My search was put on hold, or at least on the back burner as they say. My life once again became fully immersed in the ordinary world and I focused my attention on work, parenting, and graduate school. My spiritual life was limited to playing guitar and leading songs at the Catholic church we attended on Sunday. As far as I could tell, any kind of "faith healing" could be attributed to the placebo effect rather than any spiritual intervention. (I must interject, however, that currently, even with continuing research on the placebo effect, and a few theories about how it works, we ultimately don't know.)

The years went by with many changes. At the beginning of the 1991-92 school year, Wendy began a new teaching position at the American Indian Magnet School in St. Paul. This began a fascinating period of expanding and maturing on our spiritual journey. In 1993, a business partner of the Indian Magnet school donated a large medicine wheel, which was set in place on the school grounds. At the dedication ceremony something very unusual and wonderful happened which again challenged my thinking and gave me the incentive to renew my spiritual search in earnest.

As a Winnebago elder prayed with his pipe to the four directions, people around me started to look up and point toward the sky. I looked up and was filled with astonishment to see seven bald eagles above us, one following the other to form a circle in the sky. They circled until the elder finished his prayer, then flew off in different directions. There were about two hundred people present at the dedication who saw this happen. Several years later, I was working as a hospital chaplain with a nun who used to work on a reservation. When I told her about the circling eagle incident, she related how she had seen eagles fly above the mourners many times at funerals for Indigenous people on the reservation.

But this was only the beginning of the spiritual lessons. We read John G. Neihardt's *Black Elk Speaks*, Thomas Mail's *Fools Crow, Black Elk: The Sacred Ways of the Lakota*, by Wallace Black Elk and William Lyon, and several other books about Native American history and spirituality. We attended school pow wows and got to know several of the indigenous school staff. Wendy became friends with a Lakota woman who invited us to participate in two healing, or *Yuwipi*, ceremonies led by Elmer Running, a Lakota elder and *Wicasa Wakan*, or Holy Man. These ceremonies were numinous experiences, each of which opened us to new revelations in the breadth and depth of spirituality. During these ceremonies, we felt somewhat like Dorothy in the *Wizard of Oz* when she said, "Toto, I have a feeling we're not in Kansas anymore."

While these experiences didn't answer my questions about what happened with Chrissie that night years before, they showed me that the search would take me deeper and farther into the transcendent world than I ever suspected was possible. As Joseph Campbell wrote, "Beyond the veil of the known into the unknown."

As I said at the beginning of the chapter, we are all on a personal hero's journey. The stories we tell about ourselves give us clues as to which

## Chapter Two: The Journey Begins

archetypal role we play in our myth, and how that role affects our lives in general. Carl Jung began his autobiography *Memories, Dreams, Reflections* with the statement, "I have now undertaken, in my eighty-third year, to tell my personal myth."

This book is *my* attempt to tell my personal myth through the stories I share. Maybe you don't realize you're living a myth, which makes sense because your personal myth operates mostly behind the scenes, like the director on a movie set. Examining your stories can help you determine where you are on your own hero's journey and to explore what archetypal energies are working to support you, or to thwart you, on your journey. Maybe reading this book will trigger a new Call to Adventure that will help you discover more about your own personal myth and how it is influencing your life.

# Chapter Three

# *The Way of Kung Fu*

Do not look upon this world with fear and loathing.
Bravely face whatever the gods offer.
Morihei Ueshiba, The Art of Peace

It was a warm sunny afternoon in seventh grade. School had been dismissed, and I was walking across the playground and down the block to the city bus stop when a couple of infamous school bullies confronted me. They were both eighth graders—one of them, the alpha bully, was taller than me, while his "toadie" (using the designation from *A Christmas Story*) was about my size.

While the alpha bully tried to goad me into a fight, his toadie snuck behind me and got on his hands and knees just behind my legs. Once he was in place, the alpha bully pushed me and I tumbled backwards over the toadie to fall on the ground. They laughed and began kicking me from above. My feeble attempts to defend myself were valiant but ineffective, and I was getting pommeled pretty badly. Luckily, while being beset upon from above, my classmate Mike arrived on the scene and began throwing my assailants quickly and forcefully to the ground with seemingly little effort. The bullies, realizing that they were no match for Mike, expeditiously ran away. I was dumbfounded and, I might add, very happy that Mike came to my rescue. After I got up and dusted myself off, I asked him how he learned to fight like that. He told me he studied judo at the YMCA. This became another triggering event for me . . . a new call to adventure on my hero's journey, one that would lead me to a lifelong study of the Asian martial arts and healing arts.

When I got home that day, I tried to sneak past my mom to change clothes and clean up, but she saw me and interrogated me: How did my school uniform get so dirty? I quickly tried to make up some excuse she would believe—something about playing football with the guys after school—but I could tell she was not buying it. When Dad got home, she told him how I looked when I got home from school. When he asked me what happened, I embarrassingly confessed my pugilistic failure. I immediately asked him to let me take judo at the YMCA like Mike so I could learn to defend myself.

Now, driving to downtown St. Petersburg and paying money for a judo class and uniform was not an idea they jumped at right away. In fact, Dad said that he could teach me how to defend myself. That next Saturday Dad began teaching me the basics of boxing. Now, my father was a plumber and a big man, and while he was gentle and never once physically punished me or my brother, he had broad shoulders and muscular arms. He made it look easy, showing me how to block punches and cover my face, how to throw an effective punch and move around. After teaching me the basics and having me shadow box for some amount of time, he said it was time to spar so I could practice blocking punches. I don't know where he got them, but we put on boxing gloves began to spar.

Have you ever seen a cartoon when a character gets hit and stars are circling around his head? Well, that day I discovered that this didn't only happen in cartoons. At some point in our sparring, I missed a block and Dad accidentally hit me on the head. I literally saw little stars and fell to the ground. Dad quickly helped me up, apologizing profusely, and the lesson ended.

With this failed attempt at boxing, it wasn't long before Dad and Mom enrolled me in the judo classes at the downtown St. Petersburg YMCA. I suspect that Dad's guilty feelings were involved in their decision.

# Chapter Three: The Way of Kung Fu

I was excited and nervous the evening of my first judo class. I arrived at the YMCA wearing a judo *gi* (uniform) that my dad acquired from a friend who studied judo while in Japan after WWII. It was a little baggy, but Mom tailored it to fit reasonably well. Dad's friend showed me how to properly tie the white cloth *obi* (belt) around my waist. I felt very self-conscious when I stepped onto the mat-covered floor that first time, but was relieved when I saw my schoolmate, Mike. Having at least one person I knew helped me feel more comfortable. When one of the black-belted teachers called everyone to begin, Mike told me where and how to stand in line. As I stood there looking nervously around, the *sensei*, or head teacher, walked in. I was a bit confused because somehow, he looked familiar. That befuddlement quickly turned into surprise and excitement once I realized he was someone I knew: Mr. Sone.

One of my favorite places to visit on Saturday family outings was Sone's Unusual Gifts in downtown St. Petersburg. The fragrance of Japanese incense filled the air upon walking into the small store. I would slowly walk a circuit looking at and (maybe) gently touching some of the beautiful and delicate treasures neatly displayed on the shelves and in glass cases. There were Japanese lacquer pieces, silks, tea sets, vases, paper fans, lanterns, parasols, and of course, incense. After completing a leisurely exploration around the outer loop of the store, I always ended at the center, where long glass cases displayed even more expensive treasures . . . and one which contained joke gifts and magic tricks.

Mr. Sone always stood behind the glass counters, a Japanese man in his sixties who always had a ready smile. He might eagerly offer me a piece of candy from which, upon opening the box, would leap a rubber spider that would "bite" my hand. Or he might present a can of peanut brittle from which, when opened, would fly a "snake" made from a compressed, cloth-covered spring. Even though I knew this was going to happen, it always gave me a jolt. I would jump back and Mr. Sone would laugh cheerfully in delight. He would always show me a couple of simple magic tricks and I would buy one, provided I had enough money saved up from my allowance. Mr. Sone would patiently and kindly teach me how to perform the trick and praise me when I did it correctly.

Now, Mr. Taizo Sone stood in front of the class in his crisply pressed white gi with his faded black belt around his waist here at the YMCA, and I suddenly felt right at home. He would be the first teacher on my journey into the world of Asian martial arts, and I would learn even more tricks from him. Class formally began with a bow to the teachers and a prayer for our safety, after which we spent time stretching. Then I was taught how to fall backward-and roll forward safely when thrown. After that we were called to line up kneeling on the mat in formal Japanese seiza, while Sone Sensei demonstrated a throw. I could see how, through his judo mastery, he "tricked" his much taller and more muscular black belt assistants, effortlessly throwing them to the mat time after time just as Mike had done with the school bullies. His judo seemed to be just another manifestation of the magic he performed in his store. That first class had a powerful impact on me. I still remember the first throw he demonstrated that evening. It was *osoto gari* in which you step toward and to the side of your opponent, hook their leg with your leg, and twisting, throw the person to the ground. During classes, Mr. Sone was kind when correcting mistakes and quick to smile and laugh. As a Catholic school student, I took comfort in his beginning and ending class with a prayer. Sone Sensei emphasized that outside of class, we must always use judo only for self-defense. A few months later, the bullies who beat me up before confronted me again after school. The alpha bully sneered and said, "Your friend isn't here to save you now." But when he threw a punch toward my head, without thinking, I blocked it and used *ippon seoinage*, throwing my would-be assailant over my back and shoulder, catapulting him onto the concrete. He looked up from the sidewalk in shock. His toadie just stood there staring down at the dazed bully and then up at me. I simply turned around and walked away. They never bothered me again. I was only able to study judo with Mr. Sone for about a year because I was a competitive roller skater at the time and my coach was worried that I would get injured in judo and ruin my chances to compete nationally. I will always remember the way this gentle yet powerful man profoundly influenced the rest of my life. In college, I returned to the Japanese martial arts, joining the Yoshukai Karate club at Saint Leo. After graduating, I studied Hakkoryu Jiu Jitsu at the Clearwater YMCA. Sixty years have passed since those judo classes with Mr. Sone at the YMCA and I have often mused on how as a child, a magical encounter with an elderly Japanese man led to a lifelong interest in and exploration of a philosophy and practice that has so pervasively influenced my life and as a result, the lives of others.

Beginning in the fall of 1972, while still practicing jujitsu, I made sure I was always home on Thursday evenings to watch my favorite television show, *Kung Fu* with David Carradine. While the martial arts scenes were exciting and fun to watch, I mostly found myself drawn to the Taoist and Buddhist philosophy taught to the young Kwai Chang Caine by his Shaolin teachers, Master Kan and the blind Master Po in flashback scenes. Their philosophy seemed to mirror the lessons learned on the mat with Sone Sensei and now in jujitsu. Influenced by the *Kung Fu* show, I bought the book *The Wisdom of Kung Fu* by Michael Minick. Reading it led me to discover the *Tao Te Ching*, which teaches that, "The Tao never acts with force, yet there is nothing that it cannot do." (Laozi, Chapter 37, J H McDonald translation) I have tried to incorporate this philosophy not only in my martial arts training, but also in my work as a teacher, psychotherapist, emergency management coordinator, and chaplain. My spiritual and religious path has also been influenced by this philosophy. Sometimes, I refer to my spiritual path as Taoist Christian. After moving to Minnesota and beginning the doctoral program, I joined the aikido club on the University of Minnesota campus. Aikido was very similar to the jujitsu I had studied in Florida and the philosophy of its founder, Morihei Ueshiba, was very similar to that of judo and jujitsu. I soon realized however, that I was far too busy with my new job, graduate school, and a young family to spend time on the aikido mat. My martial arts journey seemed to be at an end.

In February of 1982 however, while in the midst of taking the preliminary exams for my doctoral program, I read an article in the Sunday newspaper about a man called Gin Foon Mark. He was the owner and chef at the New China Inn Restaurant in downtown Minneapolis. The focus of the article was not on Mr. Mark's cooking skills, but rather that he was a kung fu master. Master Mark had grown up in a small village near Guangdong in Southern China. He began learning kung fu from his uncle and grandfather when he was a boy of five and more formally in the local temple at age nine. In 1947 at age twenty, Mark was invited by the Chinese Association of Manhattan to teach kung fu to the Chinese community. In 1970, he moved from New York to Minneapolis. I discovered and watched a film made by the Minnesota Historical Society as part of their *Living History Series* featuring Mr. Mark titled *Kung Fu Master*. After watching this documentary, I was very excited to meet this man. So, one afternoon after work, I stopped by The New China Inn and asked a young woman who was setting tables if I could speak with Mr. Mark. She told me that he was in the kitchen prepping for the dinner crowd but she would ask him. She came back shortly and escorted me into the kitchen to meet him. He was very busy chopping onions with a Chinese cleaver. I introduced myself and told him I had read his article in the newspaper. He was very cordial and asked me if I studied any martial arts. I told him about my involvement in the Japanese martial arts since seventh grade and then I asked if he was taking any new students. He told me I should come to his school, that was next door to his restaurant and upstairs, to try it. I attended my first class at

## Chapter Three: The Way of Kung Fu

his school the following week. Shortly after I began, Master Mark came over to watch me practicing moving forward, backward, and side to side, in what he called "walking the horse." He began explaining that his art was primarily a soft or internal style of kung fu and the development of *qi* (pronounced chee) was important to learning the art correctly. He then asked me whether I believed in qi. Wanting to be honest, I told him that while I knew about it, I thought it was just a manifestation of physics and good body mechanics. He walked away and returned a short time later carrying a thick Minneapolis telephone book in his hands. Standing directly in front of me, he directed me to get into the strongest stance I knew. He told me to hold the telephone book tightly against my chest. I did as he directed, positioning myself in a karate *fudo-dachi*, or immovable stance. Master Mark placed the fingertips of one hand on the telephone book, his feet about a foot apart in no obvious stance and asked "are you ready?" I said "yes" and he quickly struck the phonebook with the palm of his hand never removing his fingertips. With a strike from that short distance, I literally flew off both feet and struck the wall behind me so hard that it knocked the breath out of me. I slid down the wall and onto the floor unable to catch my breath. Master Mark pressed a place on my back so I could breathe again. He said, "That qi. I no liar." At another class, I had a headache and Master Mark noticed how I would stop and rub my forehead during class. He came over and asked, "Headache?" Answering in the affirmative, he pressed on a couple of places on my neck with one hand and on my temples with the fingertips of his other hand. I could feel heat coming from his hand and in less than a minute the headache was gone.

As had happened with judo and aikido before, I was only able to study with Master Mark for a short period of time. Attending kung fu classes while teaching full-time, preparing for my prelims and spending time with my young children was just too much. But Master Gin Foon Mark gave me my first experience with the power of qi, this energy that he seemed to be able to summon at will and use for self-defense and for healing. It made me wonder whether qi, had been involved in my unexplainable experience with Chrissie. Once I was finished with graduate school, I signed up for a community education class to learn Cheng Man-Ch'ing's Yang Style tai chi. While tai chi has self-defense applications, the class focused on it as a practice to reduce stress and improve health.

Jumping forward a decade to the summer of 1992, Wendy and I were driving home to our condo from a camping trip on Birch Lake near Ely Minnesota. We were discussing how we would like to dedicate our lives to being a healing presence in the world. We talked about having a big enough house to offer workshops and where I could offer psychotherapy to individuals in some beautiful natural setting. Then, as Wendy was driving down Ruth Street near our home, I saw a sign on the garage door of a house that I hadn't noticed before. It reminded me of Master Gin Foon Mark's school logo. After arriving home, unpacking and relaxing for a while, I drove back there and discovered that it was indeed Master Mark's home. He was now living in St. Paul and was teaching in his garage that had been converted into his kung fu school. There was a class in session when I arrived.

As I entered the building, Master Mark greeted me. I reminded him that I had been his student ten years earlier for a short time. Nodding his head, but without commenting on whether he remembered me or not, he handed me a license plate and a screwdriver and told me to go outside and put it on his van parked in the driveway. I did so immediately, knowing that being given some trivial tasks was a common test of the prospective student's character and willingness to learn. When I was finished, I returned and told Master Mark that I didn't remember much from my previous time at his school. He responded by saying, "Your hands will remember." I told him that I was most interested in learning qigong and healing and he told me to come back on Saturday morning for qigong class.

## Chapter Three: The Way of Kung Fu

The following Saturday morning Wendy and I began what would be eight years of studying Six Healing Sounds Qigong with Master Mark. He taught in a very traditional Chinese style. He did the entire set of exercises and we students followed him as best we could. He would make comments about the correct way to do the exercise and the correct breathing as he led the routine. One of his favorite things to say was, "First I drive the car and by and by you will drive the car yourself." As well as qigong, I started attending kung fu classes and learning acupressure. Master Mark told me I should continue my tai chi practice because it was good for my health. After a little over two years of attending classes two to three times a week, Master Mark accepted me as an inner door student, or apprentice, through a traditional ceremony at the school altar.

Over my years of training with Master Mark, I tried to stop taking kung fu classes a few times telling Sifu Mark that I wanted to concentrate on qigong and healing, but he would say to develop kung fu (which literally means mastery), I had to learn all the arts: self-defense, qigong, Chinese philosophy, Chinese medicine, and calligraphy. In fact, one of the things Sifu Mark said frequently was "Everything is kung fu." His cooking is kung fu and so was Wendy's art, my psychology, and playing the piano. All are kung fu and the movement and mastery of qi energy is the basis of everything we do. When Yoda explains the Force to Luke Skywalker in *Star Wars: The Empire Strikes Back*, you could easily substitute the word qi for the Force. Yoda explains that, "Its energy surrounds us and binds us ... You must feel the Force around you, between you, me, the tree, the rock, everywhere." It would take me years of hard work to have a true understanding of the depth and power of this concept, but I have also come to realize that qi is like a fathomless well whose depths can never be fully plumbed.

One Saturday morning after qigong class, Master Mark told me he wanted to go to the University of St. Thomas to hear a doctor from Mayo Clinic lecture about acupuncture as a complementary approach to Western medicine. He suggested I pick him up and drive him there so we could both attend. On the way home from the lecture, he said he wanted me to start teaching qigong because he had been watching me and I was "strong with qi," but that I still needed to learn to control it better and use it more proficiently. This both moved and motivated me. Sometime later in my training, while I was giving Sifu a qigong healing treatment, he commented, "I like your hands." This was indeed a high compliment from a man whose usual praise was, "Not too bad."

Besides my personal daily qigong practice, I began using qigong healing methods on Wendy, my children, friends, and on the other kung fu and qigong students. In addition, Master Mark began having me lead the Saturday qigong classes at his school when he was ill or out of town. Finally, after six years of apprenticeship, Master Mark gave me a letter granting me permission to teach on my own. I began teaching a qigong class for employees of HealthEast, a large health care organization in the Twin Cities. Shortly after, Master Mark was asked to teach qigong at Northwestern Health Sciences University's School of Oriental Medicine. He said his English was not good enough and recommended me. I was hired by the University as an adjunct professor and taught a beginning and an intermediate qigong course. I was also asked to teach a course on beginning counseling skills. It seemed as though my hero's journey in this area was finished and I was bringing what I had learned on the quest to the community to help people. I would find out that the qigong journey was only taking a hiatus before it became even more intense.

One of the most important things I learned in my many years of studying Asian martial arts is that the whole world is the training school. As Sifu Mark said, "Everything is kung fu." This idea became most evident during a weeklong workshop called the Peaceful Warrior Residential Intensive that Wendy and I attended in Sonoma California. I sort of tricked Wendy into going with me. I told her that we could have a vacation in California, learn about conflict resolution and have a great time. I played down the martial arts training component, although, I honestly didn't know that we would be spending so much time practicing martial arts from early morning until late in the evening. The workshop was taught by Dan Millman, a world champion gold medalist in gymnastics, an aikido black belt, and the author of *The Way of the Peaceful Warrior*. Dan used martial arts training to help us understand how we deal with conflict and fear in our everyday life. The intensive workshop, he said, would help us to cope more effectively. We were told we would be tested at the end of the workshop in a simulated life and death situation. The workshop was strenuous physically, mentally, and emotionally. Adding to the difficulty, the weather was very hot in Sonoma that week and there was no air conditioning. Dan emphasized that the test was what we were really paying for. The techniques taught were defensive only. No counterattacks or aggression was allowed. Dan emphasized being "centered," which he defined as being in a state of simultaneous physical, mental, and emotional balance. We would learn to accept oncoming attacks while staying out of the way of danger, blending with the attacker's energy, and then redirecting it away from us. "Make it a dance" Dan would say, a metaphor that would play a major role later in my journey. Interspersed throughout the physical martial arts training, were lessons that Wendy and I have since applied to our lives.

I however, found myself struggling with the idea of being told not to use the kung fu techniques with which I was so comfortable and were so ingrained in my body. I also was becoming rankled with the idea that the staff would actually fail people. Wendy kept telling those who were worried, "They're not really going to fail anyone." My internal struggles began to manifest by being a bit too aggressive with the teachers during my practice time. I told Wendy that if she failed, I would pay back the teachers when it was my turn to test. Wendy, who was by now very into the training, saw Dan coming up behind us when I said this to her. She turned around and said to him, "Dan, tell Yanchy to stay out of my test." That evening, I was practicing with a big Swedish man who reminded me of a Viking. One of the staff came over to work with us. While practicing, I grabbed his arm and pushed him into a wall with force. He told us that if we grabbed the arm of an attacker, or pushed them away forcefully as I had just done to him, we would fail. The Swede laughed and said, "Then we will go to Valhalla." A few minutes later, Dan Millman came over to talk with us. He asked us if we could be flexible and trust the training because it was a big part of the whole experience. The idea of the training was to break out of our usual patterns of response to conflict, fear, or anger, and do something new. I felt a bit embarrassed and ashamed, and I remembered Master Mark talking about putting on the beginner's mind. A quote from the Zen teacher Shunryu Suzuki came to mind: "In the beginner's mind there are many possibilities. In the expert's mind there are few." I determined at that moment to put on a beginner's mind and do the best I could with what we were learning at the workshop and trust the training and the teachers. Wendy however, was still worried I would do something to fail the test.

The morning of the test there was very little talking after breakfast. Students sat alone or in small groups. Some smoked, some stretched, others meditated. Wendy and I sat back-to-back on a bench and did qigong breathing. Finally, as we were called into the training hall, we saw that it had been changed into a traditional Japanese style dojo. The students were directed to sit on cushions against two adjacent walls. On the opposite wall was a row of empty cushions. This was the designated area for those who failed. We were told that the test involved three instructors attacking us with rubber knives. Each teacher would attack us five times consecutively. Then the next teacher would attack, and finally, Dan would attack. We were reminded that we had to use only the techniques taught at the workshop. If we used something else, we would fail the test. If we were 'cut' or our energy was wrong, we would fail.

As the testing began I could to see how it truly did reveal how the individuals dealt with fear and conflict. Some embraced the training, stayed centered and calm, and passed. Some froze, just standing there and letting the staff 'cut' them. Others were aggressively pushing the attackers away. A few tried to run away from the staff. Even a couple of individuals with extensive martial arts training failed. I sat on my cushion observing but focusing on breathing and staying centered. Then I heard my name called out. I went to the center of the room, posed for a photo, as we had been directed, then bowed to the first teacher/attacker and took my stance. He jumped forward and shouted trying to unsettle me, but I stayed centered and ready. He moved in quickly slashing from over his shoulder and I stepped toward him but off the line of his attack, blocking with my left arm and gently guiding him with my right hand using his own momentum. He turned and immediately attacked again. I easily used another technique from the training successfully. I felt like I was in a bubble of qi. I didn't have to think, I just responded as if in a flow. I was dancing. After all fifteen attacks were finished, I returned to the middle of the room and waited. After talking among themselves, the three staff members came out on the floor and stood opposite me in a line. Dan spoke. He said, "Martial arts training doesn't always help here. We've had several very skilled martial artists fail. But in this case, it did help. That is the way it's supposed to be done. You pass." We bowed to each other and I felt a tremendous sense of relief and joy.

As I sat back down on my cushion against the wall, Wendy was on her way over to me when we heard the next name being called, Wendy Lacska. She called out, "I can't go now, not right after that." I knew how worried she had been about my test, and must be feeling a huge sense of relief, pride, and love. But Dan ignored her protest and repeated that it was her turn.

She shook herself loose and went out to the center of the room to pose for her photo. After bowing, she seemed a bit of nervous, moving back and forth from one foot to the other. Dan called out to her, "Are you centered?" She took a deep breath, exhaled, and her body relaxed somewhat. As the staff attacked her, she performed exactly as she had been trained. When it was Dan's turn to attack, he tried to unsettle her by stomping his foot and making noises, but she stayed centered and continued to meet his aggression, to block and guide him past her. On his last attack, he went across the room, got down in a runner's starting position, and ran at Wendy waving his 'knife' wildly above his head. She again performed beautifully. After that, the three instructors faced her and bowed, Dan said, "I guess it runs in the family. You pass." Wendy was so excited that she ran over to me and jumped into my lap and hugged me. When all the tests were completed, Dan spoke, directing his comments to those who had failed the test. He asked rhetorically, how many times in life have we said to ourselves, "If only I had the chance to do that over again. Today, you do have a second chance." This gave those of us who had passed, a break outside of the dojo, while those who had failed stayed with Dan and the other staff. After a while, we were all called back into the dojo and directed to again sit on our cushions against the wall. Each person who had failed the test the first time was tested and attacked three more times. As we watched it was beyond question that every one of them did much better than they had done the first time. They all passed.

This intense workshop helped me to understand that along the hero's journey one often discovers that conflicts and fearful situations are the arenas in which we are tested, strengthened, and transformed. What we learned during that week reminded me of the wisdom of the Tao Te Ching I quoted earlier in this chapter, "The Tao never acts with force, yet there is nothing that it cannot do." Morihei Ueshiba, the founder of the martial art of aikido thought of his martial art practice as the Art of Peace. He taught, "True warriors are invincible because they contend with nothing. Defeat means to defeat the mind of contention that we harbor within" (The Art of Peace). During the Peaceful Warrior Intensive, we embodied this using three words. The three words are: Accept, Blend, and Redirect. In its physical manifestation, being attacked by a replica knife, we learned to stay calm and centered and then accept the dangerous energy by actually moving toward the attacker before full power could be generated. Next, we blended with the energy by moving out of the way of its trajectory and turning to go with the flow of the potentially harmful force. Finally, we redirected the aggressive force by guiding it away from us and neutralizing the danger.

We all tend to fall back on habitual patterns of response when we feel threatened or vulnerable to negative energy. This is true whether it is physical, verbal, situational, or even from our own unconscious. Some people retreat, run away, quit, or withdraw emotionally. Others give in to the dominance or aggression of others, some confront the negative energy aggressively, either physically or verbally, until they "win." Sometimes these responses are appropriate or necessary. It may be smart to leave or run away in certain dangerous situations. Physically resisting or fighting may save our life. Arguing for something we feel very strongly about may also be appropriate. A problem occurs however, when a particular response to negative energy becomes the "go to" in all situations. Most of the responses we habitually use fall within the categories of what is called in psychology: fight, flight, or freeze generated from our primitive survival instincts. Accept, blend and redirect offer an alternative response from the more evolved rational mind.

Taoist wisdom teaches us to live a life of *wu wei*. Often translated as non-action, wu wei really means that our actions are in alignment with the natural flow of a situation. To me, wu wei is accepting, blending and redirecting. Theologian, Reinhold Niebuhr offers us a version of accept, blend, and redirect in his famous prayer:

> God grant me the serenity
> To accept the things I cannot change;
> Courage to change the things I can;
> And wisdom to know the difference.

The development of the ability to accept, blend, and redirect on my hero's journey would certainly help me to face and persevere in the face of many difficult and challenging situations.

# Chapter Four

# *The Path of the Counselor*

Any failure we could suffer throughout our lives
will turn into little successes
if we take the right path.
Keep walking.
Miguel Ángel Sáez Gutiérrez
Zori 2ª Parte

The third pathway of my hero's journey began, though unbeknownst to me, by way of my near-death experience as a child. Individuals who have an NDE are more likely to end up working in a helping profession and tend to be more empathetic and compassionate. I have clear memories of some of the young women I wanted to pursue romantically in my college years being more interested in sharing their problems and broken hearts with me rather than in seeing me as a romantic interest.

In addition to being predisposed to ending up in a helping profession by way of my NDE, the challenges of my first teaching assignment, and my feelings of inadequacy to address the challenges presented by these students, became another call to adventure on my hero's journey. On the first day on my new job, after our first staff meeting, three different teachers introduced themselves and asked if they could see my class list. One teacher just shook her head, another man laughed, and the third, the teacher of the emotionally disturbed, said it was a very challenging class and if I needed it, she would help me. On the first day of school, as I was introducing myself and explaining the classroom rules to my upper elementary and junior high aged kids, one student stood up while I was speaking and walked out of the classroom. I paused for a moment in shock and then went out to retrieve him from the drinking fountain. When I returned with that student, two others—were in a near physical fight, pushing and calling each other names. This behavior was the antithesis of my experience as a student teacher. That classroom had been filled with sweet, friendly, and compliant kids with a variety of disabilities. In this new situation however, I had no idea how to handle these kids. Not all of them exhibited behavior problems, but enough that I felt I was in the wrong profession. At the end of that first day, I talked with the teacher who had offered to help me. She gave me several suggestions that I implemented the next day. Her recommendations did help somewhat. It was this near disaster that prodded me into immediately applying for the master's degree program in working with kids who have mental health and behavioral problems at the University of South Florida. I saw this as survival training. The following September, just a few short weeks after graduating with my master's degree, I returned to teaching much better equipped to deal with these challenging students. A few years later however, when I was well on the path to earning a doctorate in educational psychology at the University of Minnesota, another pivotal and far-reaching event presented a new trial along my path.

Thinking back to high school, my undergraduate college years, and even my master's degree program, I found school pretty undemanding. I liked school and learning came easy to me. I have a good memory and can usually read something once and remember the important facts. I never really had to study very hard. I just reviewed my notes a couple of times before a test and consistently got grades of A or B. More than once as a kid, my mother would be driving me to school and I would be reviewing some notebook for a test. Mom would ask if I had a test. When I replied in the affirmative, she would ask me if I had studied. My usual reply was, "I am right now." I will admit however, I was always weaker in math and in the science classes that involved a lot of math, like chemistry and physics. But even in those classes I earned Bs in high school and scored well enough on the SAT test to receive a Florida State Board of Regents scholarship to help pay for college.

Before applying for admission to the doctoral program at the University of Minnesota, there was one hinderance that needed to be addressed. I had a glaring C on my transcript for one of my psychology classes. The professor was a proponent of child psychoanalysis, especially the theories of Melanie Klein and Bruno Bettelheim. I however, was convinced that behavioral psychology was the only way to effectively help children who were exhibiting behavioral and emotional difficulties. I openly argued with him in the seminar class. Luckily, my advisor somehow managed to get my grade changed to a B when I told her about my dilemma. Ironically, years later, I would see the wisdom and value of some of the ideas espoused by psychoanalytic theory and begin to use them in conjunction with behavioral interventions.

For the first time in my life as a student, some of the classes in my doctoral program turned out to be much more challenging than I had ever experienced in the past. I remember sitting in a couple of seminar style classes thinking that everyone else had so much more knowledge of the subject material than I had acquired. Whenever some theorist or study was mentioned that I hadn't heard of, I would go to the University library as soon as class was over and look it up. This was of course in addition to keeping up with the regular assigned readings. In class, I tried to give the impression, through timely nods of the head, that I knew what they were talking about and prayed that I would not be called upon to elucidate on the topic. Not surprisingly, this feeling of not knowing what was going on was especially true in three required classes in statistics and research. I had to constantly seek help from one of the graduate assistants to make it through the assignments and tests. With much more studying than I was used to, I finally successfully completed all of my classes with As and Bs and passed the first two of three written preliminary examinations. Then something devastating happened and I hit a proverbial wall.

I never took the last of my preliminary exams, the one in research and statistics. Even though I had passed the courses, I never really felt I had a very good grasp of this subject area. On the day of the exam, the stress of school in general, tension in my marriage, wanting to be a good dad, working full time, and my insecurity around this subject matter brought me to the breaking point and the research and statistics prelim turned out to be my coup de grâce. When I arrived on the Saturday morning of the exam, I was so filled with anxiety that I got sick, and I mean literally sick. As I entered the exam room, the anxiety overwhelmed me to such a degree, that I ran down the hall, into the men's room, and vomited. When I returned, I told the proctor that I was ill and couldn't take the exam. I went home feeling totally defeated. I couldn't even tell my wife what had happened because of my shame, knowing that telling her would have probably caused another argument.

On Monday morning I made an appointment with my advisor, Dr. Bruce Balow. We met in his office after my work day and I told him what had happened. He listened empathetically and non-judgmentally. When I finished, he offered to arrange for a tutor to help me pass the exam. But I told him that I just didn't think I could continue the program. I had reached a point where I was physically and mentally worn out. The thought of taking the statistics and research prelim, then working on a dissertation, working full time, was overwhelming. I could not afford to quit my job in order to put in the work that it would take to finish the program in the required timeframe. Dr. Balow listened attentively and asked several questions. Looking over the credits I had earned in both my master's program at the University of South Florida and there at the University of Minnesota he said I could transfer my credits to the specialist program in counseling psychology. It seemed I had enough credits, so all I had remaining was a final oral exam with a committee of three professors, all of whom I knew. This degree would still allow me to be eligible for licensure as a psychologist in Minnesota, which had become a major goal of mine. I felt a tremendous sense of relief and decided to do as he suggested. In retrospect, what Dr. Balow did that day was a perfect example of applying the accept, blend, and redirect approach, I would learn years later at the Peaceful Warrior Intensive, to the negative and stressful situation I brought to him. His empathic listening and acknowledging the difficulty of the situation I was in, was acceptance at its best. He blended by reviewing all of my credits with me and keeping in mind my goal to become licensed to practice psychology. He then skillfully redirected me to the specialist degree program.

The final oral examination was actually enjoyable. It felt more like a discussion than an examination. At one point, after responding to one of the committee member's questions, I asked another professor what he thought which engendered an interesting conversation. At the end of the exam, the committee members did not even send me out of the room to discuss it. They simply congratulated me. So, in 1982, I graduated with my specialist degree emphasizing mental health counseling. I was glad to be finished and this course of action certainly relieved a great deal of stress. Somewhere deep down however, I felt like a quitter who just didn't have the right stuff to finish a doctorate.

Joseph Campbell emphasized the importance of the role of a mentor on the Hero's Journey. He writes, "What such a figure represents is the benign, protecting, power of destiny" (The Hero with a Thousand Faces). In Greek mythology, Mentor was the friend of Odysseus who was charged with protecting and teaching his son Telemachus, while Odysseus was fighting in the Trojan War. A mentor is a more experienced person who supports and teaches us physical and technical skills, and sometimes, guides us spiritually. The mentor's role is to nudge us out of our comfort zone to answer the call to adventure. Some famous mythical mentors are Dumbledore to Harry Potter, Obi-Wan Kenobi to Luke Skywalker in Star Wars, the Oracle to Neo in the Matrix, and the goddess Athena, who ironically, disguises herself as Odysseus' friend, mentor to guide and teach Telemachus.

On my convergent paths, mentors had already appeared: Father McCall with his glow-in-the-dark crucifix talisman and religious teachings and Sone Sensei who taught me the wisdom of the soft overcoming the hard and courage in facing adversaries. But there were new mentors on this path to become a licensed psychologist, who provided me with guidance and advice. Dr. Balow had served in his role as mentor adeptly, guiding me through my coursework, and then at my most dispirited time, helping me to salvage some dignity by earning my specialist degree. After graduating, my primary supervisor throughout the required psychology internship was an indispensable mentor. He was Dr. Ralph McKinney. I knew Dr. McKinney from the Catholic Church we both attended with our families. Ralph was a nationally recognized expert in helping people who were suffering from chronic pain and illness and in the use of clinical hypnosis in psychotherapy. One of the first things Ralph did was coax me into taking the Introductory Workshop in Clinical Hypnosis offered through the University of Minnesota Medical School. Ralph was one of the teachers. I did as he suggested and was very gratified that I followed his advice. Clinical hypnosis would become a valuable and often utilized tool in my integrative counseling work. The introductory workshop set the stage for my attending several of the annually offered Advanced Clinical Hypnosis Workshops, and for joining the Minnesota Society of Clinical Hypnosis. These many years later, I still consider Ralph to be my mentor, we have become dear friends and colleagues. We still meet for lunch and consult with each other on challenging cases.

My first experience as a psychology intern was working with senior high school students who were living with chronic disease at the school where

## Chapter Four: The Path of the Counselor

I had previously taught adolescents with mental health challenges. I was fortunate to be paid for this work through a Children's Mental Health Grant that enabled me to work with these students individually and in weekly therapy groups. The school nurse also invited me to co-facilitate a grief group for students who had lost a parent, grandparent, other family member, or a friend. I was happy to do this and learn all I could about grief which would turn out to be valuable for the direction my future counseling work would take, as well as being beneficial in dealing with grief issues that would soon come into my own life. Ralph came to the high school to co-facilitate the chronic illness group the first couple of times we met. He also invited me to be a guest at his chronic pain group at the Golden Valley Pain Management Clinic. He asked me to teach the participants some of the cognitive behavior therapy techniques that had been a strong component of my graduate studies. One of the questions on my preliminary exam in psychology was to compare and contrast two influential psychologists. I chose Albert Bandura, a leading proponent of Social Learning Theory and cognitive behaviorism, and Carl Jung. I had no way to know at that time, the serendipity of this decision. Jung's theories and ideas would, over time, become more and more important in my counseling practice and to my personal growth.

As the time drew closer for taking the National Examination for Professional Practice in Psychology, I became more and more anxious and worried. The memory of my failure to take the research and statistics preliminary exam came looming up and I was very unsure about this area of the exam. Acting on the recommendation of a friend who had recently passed the exam, I purchased a packet of study materials that included practice questions. Somehow and in some way, something in my brain clicked as I was studying and finally, I had a working grasp of the psychological research and the statistics used in that research. So, in 1985, I passed the national psychology exams and was licensed as a psychologist in Minnesota. Mixed with my joy and relief, however, there was a sense of defeat and melancholy regarding my failure to complete the doctoral program. Earning a PhD became my personal Holy Grail, and like the Round Table knight Percival, I had failed on my first attempt to fulfill my quest. Akin to Percival, who wandered for years trying to find the Grail Castle again and rectify his failure, my own failure would always be in the shadowy background of my psyche haunting me until I too could rectify my failure.

As I continued as a psychologist, the scope of my work broadened with time and experience, and I expanded my knowledge and skills in several different capacities and settings. I worked as a part-time counselor at the Hennepin County Juvenile Detention Center, and later, as a psychotherapist at the Scott County Mental Health Center. There, my counselees expanded beyond children and adolescents and my work included helping adults through depression, phobias, anxiety, and coming to terms with their sexual identity. It was while working in Scott County that I joined the Minnesota Jung Association and began to incorporate Jung's ideas, especially dream work, into my practice. I continued to utilize cognitive behavior therapy, especially the theories of psychiatrist William Glasser, in conjunction with Jung's Depth Psychology. I first became acquainted with Dr. Glasser's work when I read his book, *Reality Therapy*, while working on my master's degree. Since then, I have read all of his books and attended several of his lectures and workshops, until his death in 2013. At one workshop, he commented that if someone has a question, they want to ask a famous person, they should put aside their fear and contact that person. I took his advice to heart, and over the years, corresponded with Dr. Glasser now and again. He would always graciously and thoughtfully answer my questions.

While working in these various capacities, I continued in my position at the Saint Paul Schools at least part-time, I was assigned to the Staff

Development Department and provided workshops on stress management, applying Glasser's theories in the classroom, psychological first aid, crisis management, and other topics. Then, due to the proliferation of school shootings around the nation, I was hired through a Homeland Security/FEMA grant, as the full-time emergency preparedness coordinator for the St. Paul Public Schools. Because of the funding source through FEMA, I worked closely with the St. Paul Police and Fire Departments and the Minnesota Department of Homeland Security and Emergency Management. I traveled around the state, conducting workshops on school safety, as well as training school psychologists, social workers, counselors, and nurses in psychological first aid and crisis intervention and conducting threat assessments. During those years, I was also invited to lecture on school safety at conferences in Washington DC and I was a participant in the school safety conference at which a group of experts met with president George W. Bush, his wife Laura, and representatives from the Department of Education and Homeland Security to make recommendations for the federal government's role in the school safety crisis. I became certified in Critical Incident Stress Debriefing and served as a member of the Minnesota Emergency Management Mental Health Task Force. In addition, I taught as an adjunct professor in the Graduate Continuing Studies Department at Hamline University in St. Paul. By most standards and in most people's eyes, I had become a very successful and skilled professional. And yet, I had an underlying dissatisfaction because of my failure to finish my doctorate those many years before. A few times over the years, I explored various doctoral programs, but as I continued to evolve and transform, finding a program that suited me became more and more difficult because I was no longer willing to sit through classes in which I had no interest. Other adventures and mentors would soon appear in my life that would help me wend my way along the twisting paths of my personal hero's journey and quest for my personal grail.

# Chapter Five

# *The Dark Night of the Soul*

> Midway upon the journey of our life
> I found myself within a forest dark,
> For the straightforward pathway had been lost.
> Ah me! How hard a thing it is to say
> What was this forest savage, rough, and stern,
> Which in the very thought renews the fear.
> Dante's Inferno - Canto 1

As a thirty-five-year-old man, while winding up all the requirements for my license to practice psychology, I was about to find myself, like Dante, in a dark forest. I was about to experience what the sixteenth century Spanish monk and mystic John of the Cross termed, the "Dark Night of the Soul."

When we, in our Western culture, hear the term "dark" or "darkness," we tend to think of something evil or malevolent, such as the "dark side of the force" in Star Wars or the "Dark Lord" in the Harry Potter books and films. This was not however, the intention of John of the Cross. The Spanish word he used for dark was *oscura*, which means obscure, as in how something is difficult to see at night or inside of a cave. During a vacation and pilgrimage to the Island of Iona, Wendy and I attended the evening worship service. After the service ended, we began walking back to our room at the Argyll Hotel. We had to cross a field to get to the dirt road leading to the little town and the hotel. We quickly discovered that the night was so dark that we couldn't even see the ground beneath our feet. We felt stuck and worried that we would not be able to find our way back to our hotel. This is the kind of dark that John of the Cross was referring. The dark night of the soul refers to an inability to see our way clearly; to feel stuck and lost.

My dark night began in February of 1985 when my father had a heart attack and was in the hospital. I talked with him on the telephone telling him I was flying down to Florida to be with him. He talked me out of it, saying that I should wait until he was out of the hospital and relaxing at home. We could then, he reasoned, better enjoy out time together. I reluctantly agreed. Then sadly, while he was still in the hospital, Dad had a second heart attack that was fatal. He was seventy-two years old when he died. I flew to Florida as soon as I was able to get a flight, so that I could be with my mother and my brother, and to help with the funeral arrangements. Mom was grief-stricken to lose the man she loved dearly and to whom she had been happily married for forty-four years, since December 8,1941, the day after the Japanese bombed Pearl Harbor. While, I too was shocked and sad, I remained emotionally in control to support Mom. Somehow, I didn't cry, except a few quiet tears, during the funeral and the whole time I was in Florida. I just felt numb.

Only a few days after returning home and to work, I co-facilitated the grief group for senior high school students with the school nurse. During the group session, I suddenly felt overwhelmed with grief and excused myself because I was worried that if I stayed, I would break down emotionally in front of the students. I felt tremendous anxiety and sadness, but I still did not cry. A few weeks later, I had the following dream. I am visiting my parent's home in Florida. Mom, Dad, and my brother are all there. In my dream I have a lucid moment, and think, *How can Dad be here, He's dead?* All of a sudden, all of the images in the dream disappeared, except for my dad. He says to me, "Of course I'm here. I will always be with you." I woke up and wept, sobbing in sorrow, grief, and love for several minutes. This release of emotions provided me with a feeling of relief and catharsis. I still felt, however, a deep sense of regret for not following my intuition and fly

## Chapter Five: The Dark Night of the Soul

down to see Dad immediately as I had originally planned. If I had done this, I would have been able to talk with him and touch him one last time. It is a regret that I carry in my heart.

Six months after my dad's death, there was another family tragedy. My brother Paul caught a respiratory virus and was admitted to the hospital because he was having difficulty breathing. He died from a pulmonary embolism leading to heart failure. My brother Paul was only forty years old and left behind his wife a teen-aged daughter and a son. My mother was devastated to have lost both her husband and her oldest son in such a short time span. I was now her only living child, and found myself in Florida again, supporting my mom, sister-in-law, niece and nephew, and helping plan another funeral. It was a very difficult time. At the funeral, I discovered what a good man my brother had become. Several people approached me and told stories of how he helped them to get a start in some business. A couple of months later, I returned to Florida to check up on Mom and to support her. I took her to the doctor for a physical and to review her medications. After the doctor visit, we went to Mom's favorite Chinese restaurant. As we were enjoying our meal, I proposed that she move to Minnesota. She could live with us until we found a nice apartment near our house so we could help her as she aged. She listened, paused, and thanked me. Then, putting down her cutlery, she made it crystal clear that she had no intention of leaving her home in Florida where she and Dad had lived for so many years. When I laid out the reasons why it was a good idea to move, she quickly asserted her maternal authority saying, "I am the mother and you are the child. You don't tell me what to do, I tell you what to do. And I'm telling you to go back up north and I am staying here." My brother's teenage daughter, Dawn, moved in with Mom, relieving most of my worry about her living alone.

Mom enjoyed having two of her grandchildren nearby. She also had coffee every day with my Aunt Grace and we talked on the phone regularly, but her life would not return to any sense of normality after Dad and my brother Paul died. She no longer slept in the bed she had shared with Dad saying it was just too sad. Instead, she slept in her recliner chair in the living room, where she could look at the little altar she had set up on a shelf in the corner. On it was the urn with Dad's ashes, a photo of him in his WWII Army Air Corps uniform, his rosary beads, and a small vase that was always filled with fresh flowers.

Two years after Dad died, on Holy Thursday 1987, Mom also passed away. She died from a stroke in the home she loved. Again, I found myself on a flight back to Florida to arrange another funeral. I had to meet with my parent's attorney to deal with Mom's will, meet with her life insurance agent, and close her bank account, which we had the foresight of making a joint account with me after my brother died. The house needed to be thoroughly cleaned and cleared out, and I had to hire a realtor to sell it. Thankfully, relatives and some of my old high school friends came to help. My wife at the time, Ann, was a big help. This was probably the closest we had been emotionally for some time. She took charge of the house cleaning which was necessary, in my befuddled, grieving state. I went through all of Mom and Dad's belongings, and doing this in such a short period of time was extremely stressful and sad. I gave away things that I regretted losing later. Mom had asked me to make sure that both her and Dad's ashes were poured out together into the Gulf of Mexico, which I did with a sense of honor and sadness. Upon returning home to Minnesota, I felt very alone and sad. The loss of all the members of my immediate family, within such a short period of time, gave rise to serious reflection on my own mortality. I fell into a deep period of grief. I could not find any solace in the Catholic church that we continued to attend and other churches that I explored also lacked what I was looking for, although, I didn't really know what I was searching for. It seemed that the comfortable ideas about God I had from my childhood, no longer worked for me. So, adding to my grief, it seemed as though God had abandoned me too.

## Chapter Five: The Dark Night of the Soul

I had several powerful dreams during this time of the dark night. In one dream, I was facing a knight clad in red armor. He handed me his sword and then took out his dagger. He attacked me and we began to fight. I defended myself effectively, but I could not get the advantage. So, I began to attack more aggressively. When I did this, he cut my hand and laughed. The harder I tried to defeat him, the more I would get cut. Later that same night I had the same basic dream, but this time my adversary was a Red Ninja. The same scenario played out. When I woke up, I looked up the symbolism of the Red Knight in Emma Jung's and Marie-Louise von Franz's book, *The Grail Legend*. In the legend, the Red Knight stole a cup from King Arthur and was challenged and killed by the young innocent boy, Percival, who takes the Red Knight's armor and becomes the Red Knight himself. According to Emma Jung and von Franz, the Red Knight is a symbol for the Shadow. During my dark night of the soul, I was becoming more aware of the aspects of myself that had been hidden in the shadowy realms of my unconscious. All those elements that I viewed as bad, unacceptable, or flawed began to surface. My ego and personas seemed to be fighting for control. In depth psychology, the ego helps us stay grounded in the conscious part of the psyche and in the outside world. The ego wants stability and safety, and engenders this by categorizing and organizing both the outside and our inner world. In doing this however, the ego can become rigid, and resistant to change. Wendy jokes that I have a Mr. Carson, the butler from Downton Abbey, inside of me, and he likes to come out every once and awhile to make sure things are proper and following convention. My Mr. Carson comes out whenever we attend a funeral and some people are dressed far too casually. In trying to keep order, the ego can neglect or suppress other parts of the psyche, like our instinctual drives, banning them into the shadow.

Facing the Red Knight and Ninja in my dream was an indication that my shadow was challenging my ego's control. The shadow was trying to free my repressed unconscious attributes, so that my ego could learn to relate to these shadowy components in healthier ways instead of being overwhelmed by them when they surface. As Jung wrote in his book, *Psychology and Alchemy*, "There is no light without shadow and no psychic wholeness without imperfection." I needed to integrate my shadow into my conscious self and not keep trying to "defeat" him. I would later learn to accept, blend, and redirect my shadow, with outside conflicts and stressors. My ego and shadow had to learn to work together like yin and yang, in order for me to become a balanced and whole person.

Another version of the dark night of the soul in myth and story is called the Night Sea Journey. In the 2018 Warner Brothers film, *Aquaman*, which is a classic hero's journey, Arthur (aka Aquaman), and his companion, Princess Mera, must go on a night sea journey on a stormy sea to discover the abyss in which they can find and recover a magical trident, that is suspiciously like Poseidon/Neptune's Trident. Only by winning the trident, can Aquaman realize his true purpose as King of Atlantis. Other versions of the night sea journey appear in Matthew's gospel story of Jesus calming a storm on the Sea of Galilee, Jonah and the whale, and the tragedy of Captain Ahab's unresolved night sea journey in Herman Melville's *Moby Dick*.

Not only did my grief immerse me in the dark night, but physical pain brought me deeper into the abyss. Later, the summer that my brother died, we were vacationing at my wife's brother's lake home. I was water skiing on one ski, when suddenly my ski hit a sand bar causing me to abruptly jerk to a stop. I let go of the tow rope handle but inertia drove my body forward and face first into the sand just missing my ski. After the initial shock and pain, I seemed to be okay except for some abrasions on my face from the sand. The next morning however, when I tried to get out of bed, my back hurt so much that it took several minutes just to maneuver myself into a position that would allow me to sit up. The slightest movement caused wrenching pain in my lower back which made walking difficult.

## Chapter Five: The Dark Night of the Soul

The twelve-hour drive home did not help. When the pain didn't resolve after several days, my doctor ordered a CT scan that revealed I had two herniated discs in my lower back. He referred me to physical therapy and prescribed high doses of a non-steroidal anti-inflammatory drug. Those interventions helped lesson the pain, but my stomach soon could not tolerate the medication, so I had to discontinue it. I tried acupuncture, massage, and chiropractic. Some of these treatments offered temporary relief, but within a few weeks, I would have another long episode of incapacitating pain. A spine surgeon told me that surgery would only offer a fifty percent chance of resolving the problem. I didn't like those odds, so for the next ten years, I had reoccurring bouts of debilitating back pain.

During this dark time, I had two other dreams that were a variation of the night sea journey. As the first dream begins, I am piloting a WWII Mitchell B-25 Bomber over an ocean. Two other crew members are with me, a co-pilot and a radio operator/navigator; neither of whom I knew in waking life. It is nighttime and the aircraft engines begin to sputter and then stop. We go down into the ocean close to an island. As we hit the ocean, the plane skitters across the water, comes to a stop, and slowly begins to sink. We get out of the airplane and swim ashore. Once on shore we follow a jungle path and soon arrive at a large open area with a grand old Victorian mansion, replete with a manicured yard and gardens. There are many adults and children all dressed as costumed characters from fairy tales, literature, and myths. Someone greets us and shows us to a table with an assortment of delicious looking food and beverages. We refresh ourselves and look around at the people playing games or gathering in groups talking. All of them seem to be acting out the role of the character they have assumed. A woman in a white classical Greek style gown greets us and tells us that we must choose characters to become while we are there and then we will be happy and content. We decide to become the Three Musketeers. After putting on the appropriate costumes, we join in the fun.

After a while, I decide to leave the party and explore the island. But as I attempt to leave the grounds, a big and muscular bald man stops me and says that I cannot leave because it would be too dangerous. We argue and when I try to get past him, he grabs my arm, physically trying to stop me. The woman in the Greek gown intervenes and takes me aside to talk with me. I don't remember what she said. Then I awaken.

As I analyze this dream, several ideas come to mind. It begins as the classic night sea journey. Being with two other members of my crew introduces the number three in the dream. Three is a sacred number in many cultures, so the three members of the crew informs me that this is a spiritual dream. The Victorian mansion and gardens as a setting for the dream calls to mind the strict code of behavior and societal expectations of the Victorian era. If I simply follow the rules, I will be happy and safe. Everyone having to choose a character to portray is a nod to the persona. The original meaning of the term persona is mask, so our personas are the masks we wear in public, in order to present a particular image. I have worn the persona of the good son, the athlete, the father, the psychologist, and others. When I was first licensed as a psychologist, I wore a beard, a tweed sports coat with leather patches sewn on the sleeves, and smoked a pipe. This was my image of the psychologist persona. Carl Jung wrote that, "Every calling of profession, for example, has its own characteristic persona … One could say, with a little exaggeration, that the persona is that which in reality, one is not, but which oneself as well as others think one is" (CW). When I attempt to leave my persona behind in the dream to explore the island (the unknown parts of my psyche), my ego tries to keep me safe by stopping me.

A few months later, I had the second dream. I am again flying at night in a B-25, and again we crash in the sea and swim to shore, just as in the first dream. People are again all taking on the roles of fairytale, mythological, or literary characters. The woman in the white Greek gown tells me I must choose a character to become and then I'll be happy. But this time, I refuse.

## CHAPTER FIVE: THE DARK NIGHT OF THE SOUL

The scene immediately changes and I'm walking on the other side of the island on a white sandy beach. A small row boat is pulled up on shore. I see and explore the ruins of a Greek or Roman style temple. There is a bonfire burning in the courtyard of its remains. No one else is around. I look across the water, and in the distance, I see a beautiful island that is glowing with a bluish light. I want desperately to go there but the water is very rough with high waves. I'm afraid, but I push the small boat into the water, get into it, and begin to row toward the island. Soon water begins to come in over the sides of the small boat. I'm afraid that it will sink and I will drown. I wake up. This second dream seemed to be telling me that I will no longer have a satisfying and meaningful life if I continue to only live out the personas and social masks that I project to those around me. Jung believed that this awareness is the time when the individuation process can begin in earnest. The growth, or individuation process, is frightening. As I was in my dream, everyone on the night sea journey will be afraid. After all, they may drown and there are monsters in the shadowy dark depths.

One of the most challenging aspects of the dark night of the soul is that it often arises from the breakdown and collapse of what has been known and steady in one's life. In addition to my grief and chronic back pain, my marriage was dying. In public, we wore the personas of a happily married couple, but as soon as we would leave an event or someone's home, we would begin arguing. It seemed as though we disagreed about almost everything and we fought regularly. We attempted marriage counseling twice, but the years of disagreement and my feelings of loneliness and anger were too much to overcome. Our marriage ended in divorce.

With the help of a skilled psychotherapist, I was able to move through my grief, the breakdown of my marriage, and my existential crisis, and began to heal. The experiences and comfort of what the ego had built up were tumbling down and that which was lurking in the shadows of my unconscious was revealing itself. Existential and spiritual questions arose and I asked myself, *what is the meaning of life?* and *What is my purpose?* With the help of my therapist, I also discovered that the dark night not only involved suffering, but was a time of self-discovery. It forced me to see things I would have ordinarily overlooked. The dark night, or night sea journey, is an alchemical time; a time of transition and rebirth. In the gospel of Thomas, Jesus says, "If you bring forth what is within you, what you bring forth will save you. If you do not bring forth what is within you, what you do not bring forth will destroy you." Just as we were stuck in the dark and couldn't find our way that night on Iona, suddenly a gentleman with a torch as he called it, appeared and guided us to the road leading back to our hotel. Like this man did physically that night on Iona, new mentors would appear in my life and help me find my way out of the dark woods.

The following dream reassured me that my dark night would indeed come to an end. In my dream, I enter a large cave. Inside, there were torches ensconced in the walls, dimly lighting the cave and casting undulating shadows against the rock walls. As I cautiously advanced into the cave, I was met by Death, who was dressed in the classic long black hooded robe and carrying a staff. I could not see a face inside the hood, motioning with his staff, Death spoke, telling me to follow him. As we continued, the cave became more like a series of rooms in a big haunted castle with stone walls. I was very frightened at first but became less so as we continued. I came to the realization that nothing there could really harm me, only scare me. Once I realized this, Death transformed, turning into a tall and beautiful woman with golden hair, wearing a white Greek or Roman style gown with a golden belt and cape. She was an archetype of the goddess. She invited me to kiss her, but I became frightened again, thinking, *This is how Death will claim me. If I kiss her, I will die.* But ignoring my fear, I kissed her on her cheek and the dream ended. In this dream, the cave seemed to symbolize the dark night of the soul in which I had entered. Death personified was very real in that it had claimed my father, mother, and only brother, and also represented the death of my marriage and the chronic back pain that had killed much of my youthful athleticism. The dream ended with an assurance that the dark night and its shadows will soon be coming to a conclusion with the aid of a goddess, who I continued to encounter in my dreams, and who I would soon meet as a very real person in my everyday awake life.

We all face sadness, illness, death and grief. These experiences and their accompanying emotions, bind us together as humans. It is important to recognize the difference between the dark night, grief, clinical depression, and post-traumatic stress disorder (PTSD). The dark night can certainly include elements of all of these but it is not the same. A clinically depressed person has a serious loss of energy. It is often difficult to even get out of bed in the morning. The usual enjoyment found in being with friends, in hobbies, and even in sexual relations is lost. In contrast, the dark night involves a questioning of one's meaning and purpose in life and an inability to connect with the Divine. However, individuals experiencing the dark night have the feeling that somehow, spiritually, there is deep down, some meaning to be gleaned from this suffering. It is important to have a skilled psychiatrist or psychotherapist to help work through depression. A pastoral counselor or a spiritual director can be very helpful in working through the dark night of the soul.

In our Western culture, we usually reject suffering as having no value and as something to avoid if at all possible. Of course, we must treat illness and pain with the appropriate medical and complementary interventions. Often when an individual experiences grief or situational depression, the first response is too often, to fight it, repress it, or medicate it with pharmaceuticals, street drugs, or alcohol. You can probably recall numerous films and novels in which a person's first response to the death of someone close, or to the breakup of a relationship, is to get drunk. I have witnessed too many times, a grieving loved one quickly being offered a prescription drug to help them feel better by a well-meaning doctor or friend. Perhaps the best prescription for most grief is to grieve. Jungian analyst, James Hollis. in his book, *Living an Examined Life: Wisdom for the Second Half of the Journey* wrote the following:

> There is no going forward without a death of some kind; A death of who we thought we were and were supposed to be; a death of a map of the world we thought worthy of our trust and investment; a death of expectations that by choosing rightly we could avoid suffering, experience the love and approval of those around us, and achieve a sense of peace, satisfaction arrival home. But life has other plans it seems; indeed, our own souls have other plans.

In Buddhist teachings, the first noble truth is often inaccurately translated into English as "Life is suffering." But the word *dukkha*, literally refers to a wheel that is off center on its axis. So, dukkha might more accurately refer to a life that is off-kilter, or of wandering without purpose. I am convinced that I needed to go through the dark night of the soul in order to discover my true self and continue my hero's journey. Irish poet and author Dylan Morrison writes, "The darkness from which we try to escape may often be the portal to the Light of Divine Love. Best let the Source draw us through it in its own Way and Time."

# Chapter Six

# *Meeting the Goddess*

*The dark night of the soul comes just before revelation.
When everything is lost, and all seems darkness,
then comes a new life and all that is needed.*
**Joseph Campbell**
*L'amor che move il sole e l'altre stelle*
(The love that moves the sun and the other stars)
**Dante Alighieri, Paradiso**

As Joseph Campbell notes in *Reflections on the Art of Living*, quoted above, "When everything is lost, and all seems darkness, then comes the new life and all that is needed." This often happens at the stage of the hero's journey Campbell refers to as Meeting the Goddess. This goddess encounter appears time and again in myths, fairy tales, literature, and in film. She may appear as a classical goddess, like Athena who helps Odysseus on his wanderings, or the good witch Glinda who helps Dorothy in *The Wizard of Oz*, or the Elf Queen, Galadriel who helps Frodo on his quest in *The Lord of the Rings*. But this archetypal goddess may also be an ordinary woman who aids and supports the hero on the quest and with whom a strong bond of love ensues, either over time, or immediately. This love sometimes manifests as the kind of love a mother has for her child, as it does in George McDonald's book, *The Princess and the Goblin*, between twelve-year-old princess Irene and the mysterious and beautiful lady who identifies herself as Irene's great-great-grandmother. In other stories, this love between the goddess and the hero blooms into the joining of two souls in a romantic and sacred marriage as it does for Arwen and Aragorn in *The Lord of the Rings*. In any telling of the story however, the meeting with the goddess is the turning point of the hero's journey.

My favorite Children's book is *The Enchanted Wood*. This original fairy tale, written and beautifully illustrated by Ruth Sanderson, is a wonderful example of the hero's journey. Sanderson begins by telling her readers that the queen has died, and the king and even the land, are in grief. This grief is causing drought and the kingdom is becoming a wasteland. As is a typical storyline in many fairy tales, the king sends his oldest son on a quest. He must find the tree at the "Heart of the World" that, "lies beyond the mountains, in the Enchanted Wood." Only this magical tree can break the curse of sadness and save the land. The eldest son goes on the quest but does not return. After some period of time, the second son rides off to save the kingdom but also fails to return. Finally, the king reluctantly agrees to allow his youngest son, Galen, to seek the Heart of the World. When Galen arrives at the gate to the walled Enchanted Wood, he is greeted by an elder woman who holds the key to the gate. Unlike his arrogant brothers who dismissed the woman's advice in their hubris, Galen responds politely to the woman and is invited to rest in her cottage for the night. The next morning, as Galen is about to leave on his quest, the wise woman gives him the following advice, "Be true to the quest, at any cost. Stray from the path, and you will be lost." The woman's beautiful daughter, Rose, with her mother's blessing, joins Galen on his quest. Along the path, Galen is tempted to leave the path twice, to save each of his brothers. But Rose, who acts in the archetypal figure of the goddess, reminders him to stay on the path or he too will be cursed and the quest will fail. The couple successfully find the tree at the Heart of the World and save the kingdom. Of course, as in any good fairy tale, Galen rescues his brothers and many others who have been lost in the Enchanted Wood. The wise woman and Rose come to live at his father's castle, where in due time, Galen marries Rose and is crowned as the new king with Queen Rose at his side.

Meeting a goddess was not something that I knew about during this time on my journey. I had met an older wise woman in the guise of

## Chapter Six: Meeting the Goddess

my psychotherapist, but she was far more teacher and mentor than a mythical goddess. The goddess archetype appeared again in a dream during my dark night. In my dream, a woman in a long white gown gives me a gift. The gift is a beautiful wooden box with gold hinges and hasp. Upon opening it, I see that it contains square white tiles with different colored rune-like symbols on them. I think they somehow indicated different places I had been or would go and that she would add to them as necessary. I tell her I think the gift is far too valuable and ask why she is giving it to me. She smiles and kisses me on the forehead. I jump back surprised. She then says to me, "We love you." I reply, "But I am in love with, and true to Wendy." She laughs and says, "Not a love like that."

From the time I was a young man, I thought I had some kind of emotional or spiritual flaw that manifested as an inability to love a woman in the way romantic lovers did in myth, film, and literature. Of course, I had girlfriends and enjoyed being with them and was certainly sexually attracted to them, but I never really felt strong romantic feelings. It was as if my heart was deficient in some way. In my college psychology classes, I had read the "experts" who proclaimed that romantic passionate love was just an initial hormonal response that would mellow over time to become what they defined as "mature love." I had observed that some couples I knew lived together more like roommates than romantic partners. At the time, I assumed that these experts were correct,—as that—was the kind of relationship I was experiencing my own marriage. After my own meeting with the goddess, I wondered if those experts were just rationalizing because of the lack of sustained romantic feelings in their own intimate relationships. Somewhere, however, deep in my psyche and hidden in my heart, I longed for a romantic love relationship. For years prior to my divorce, I had frequent dreams in which I was happily married to someone and then, in a lucid moment, would remember in my dream that I was married to someone else in my awake life. When the song, "Somewhere Out There," sung by Linda Ronstadt and James Ingram began to be played on the radio, I would feel sad and would wonder if "Somewhere out there, someone's saying a prayer, that we'll find one another, in that big somewhere out there."

I met the goddess of my hero's journey at work. I know that doesn't conjure the image of a magical place to encounter a goddess, but my hero's journey, like most people's, was playing out in my everyday life and not on a journey to some far away or magical land. Of course, I have mentioned my goddess many times in this book. My goddess is Wendy. We met when we were both assigned to put together a workshop for teachers, administrators, and support staff like school social workers, nurses, and psychologists in the school district where we both worked. I was still in the dark night of the soul, having only recently lost my dad, mom, and brother a very few years earlier, and had recently separated from my wife. Wendy and I got along very well at work and we quickly became friends. She was dating a couple of guys and I was just sorting out my life in a studio apartment and having my kids stay with me every other weekend. Neither of us had any romantic thoughts about the other, but we empathically listened to each other and offered suggestions for dealing with our adolescent teens going through their own difficulties at the time. We discovered we were both reading Dan Millman's *The Way of the Peaceful Warrior*, and we were both watching the Public Television replay of *The Power of Myth*, in which Bill Moyers was interviewing Joseph Campbell. We both loved the film *Field of Dreams*, a film that no matter how many times I watch it, when Ray says, "Hey Dad, you want to have a catch?" I still cry. As our friendship grew, we continued to discover many common interests, ways of thinking, and experienced many synchronicities.

The goddess in myth and fairy tale is often associated with the natural world. Synchronistically, when we started working together, Wendy told

## Chapter Six: Meeting the Goddess

me about how she had just hiked down the Yosemite John Muir Mist Trail that previous summer and brought photos for all of our officemates to see. She also loved the North Shore of Lake Superior, a place I also enjoyed. After we became friends, we would often go to the Como Park Conservatory and allow the plants and water to renew us after a busy and stressful work day. The goddess in the hero's journey is also described as loyal, unselfish, and steadfast. She provides the hero with emotional and practical support by nurturing and guiding him. She is decidedly feminine, yet also emanates sensuality and strength. Over time, I would discover that Wendy had all of these qualities. Something happened however, that changed our relationship and in mythical terms, I encountered the goddess in her.

As our first workshop date became imminent, we decided to work on a Saturday at Wendy's condominium. While there, seemingly out of the blue, I had to fight back a strong desire to kiss her. I told myself, "You can't do that. You will ruin your friendship." Once I resolved not to risk our friendship with a kiss, a deep sadness overshadowed me. Wendy could see that I was troubled, and thinking I was sad because of a recent problem with one of my children, said, "You need a hug." She put her arms around me in a compassionate but completely platonic manner. I felt a strong feeling in my heart, touched her chin, raised her head to face me, and kissed her. I could feel a powerful energy open my heart. She later told me that when I kissed her, she felt her knees buckle beneath her, like in the old movies of the 1930s and 40s. To borrow from *The Princess Bride*, "Since the invention of the kiss there have been five kisses that were rated the most passionate, the most pure. This one left them all behind." Joseph Campbell explained, "The heart is the organ of opening up to somebody else… it is the opening of the heart." In his *Red Book*, Jung wrote that he found his soul again "only through the soul of the woman." And it was through meeting Wendy, the goddess in my life, that I could open my heart and find my soul again. My heart, that had seemed closed and locked, was thrown open by that magical kiss.

Meeting with the Goddess on the hero's journey usually involves a test of the hero's worthiness to succeed on the quest. I didn't know this at the time, but mythically, the favor of the goddess can only be attained by the hero proving their virtue. There is always some kind of test to appraise the hero's moral character. My test, although I didn't know it at the time, occurred the day after our kiss. I called Wendy on the phone and she answered cooly and abruptly said, "What do you want?" I answered from my now opened heart, "I'll tell you what I don't want. I don't want a sexual affair. I just want to see where our relationship takes us naturally." She was open to this idea. Shortly after this, I found an obscure poem by Kahlil Gibran, that I wrote an abridged version of, on a blank greeting card. During a coffee break at work, I pushed it across the cafeteria table in front of Wendy saying nothing. It read:

> Life carries us hither and thither and destiny moves us from one place to another. We see not, save the obstacle in our path; neither do we hear, save a voice that makes us to fear. Love passes us by clothed in the robe of gentleness and we are afraid and hide in dark caves. Truth visits us led by the smile of a child and a lover's kiss and we close the door of our tenderness against her and abandon her as one unclean. And when one hears the cry of his heart and the call of the spirit, we say such a one is possessed of a madness. The days meet us and we fear the days and the nights. How sweet to us is life and how far we are from life.

After Wendy finished reading it, she closed the card, looked out the window with tears in her eyes and touched my hand.

The appearance of the goddess on the journey is a sign from the Divine Spirit that the seeker is on the right path and has not been defeated by the dark night. As Arwen tells Aragorn in the *Lord of the Rings* film, "The Shadow does not hold sway yet, not over you, not over me." The goddess is the ultimate hope, guiding, supporting, loving and assuring that the

## Chapter Six: Meeting the Goddess

hero will complete the quest. The ultimate adventure comes, like in *The Enchanted Wood*, through the marriage of the hero and the goddess. This is a mystical marriage in which the hero and the goddess experience a love that is the sacred union of two souls, a bonding that gives the hero the courage to complete the quest. And courage is the perfect word to use here. The word comes from the Latin and French word meaning heart.

As I write this chapter, Wendy and I have been together for 31 years. We share a life of intimacy, love, romance, joy, and true companionship. She has guided me, supported me, loved me, and assured me along the way, and I have done the same for her. After all these years, if we run into each other unexpectedly in a store, our hearts still tingle with a joy that brings smiles to our faces. In addition to our strong feelings of love, we have a shared sense of purpose. One example of this is the story I shared in chapter three of how a year after we were married, Wendy and I were talking about dedicating our lives to bringing healing to people. We fantasized about having a bed and breakfast in a beautiful natural setting, where people could stay, eat healthy food, and I could offer workshops and counseling. We decided that we should spend the next few years exploring this. We never did buy a Bed and Breakfast, although we have opened up our home to people for qigong classes, retreats, and spiritual gatherings and I do see individuals here for counseling. As I think about the dreams, I had of the mystery woman to whom I was married, I now believe that it was Wendy, and I think again about the lyrics of the song from *An American Tail*: "Somewhere out there if love can see us through, then we'll be together, somewhere, out there, out where dreams come true."

Our wedding announcement included a quote from Pierre Teilhard de Chardin. It was a foreshadowing of what was to come in our marriage. "Love alone is capable of uniting living beings in such a way as to fulfill them, for it alone takes them and joins them by what is deepest in themselves." Reflecting back on the idea that romantic love would simmer down into 'mature' love, I guess our love has always been both romantic and mature. It seems to meet the definition of what psychologist Erich Fromm calls mature romantic love. Fromm asserts that a mature romantic love is one in which two individuals are joined together in an intimate sensual relationship that at the same time encourages each partner to maintain their uniqueness and individual sense of identity. This love allows for both sacred union and separation at the same time. Mature romantic love is a paradox in which two become one and yet remain two. I wrote in my Journal in 1995:

> I want to remind myself—always remind myself and keep these thoughts close to my consciousness: Only a little more than four years ago, I believed there was something wrong with me—that I really couldn't love romantically and that I would never find someone who would love me the way I desired to be loved. I was ready to live a life without that kind of love. Now I have Wendy in my life and I have more love and feel more love than I ever thought, or fantasized, was possible.

# Chapter Seven

# The Paths Begin to Converge

Kiss a lover
Dance a measure,
Find your name
And buried treasure...
Face your life
Its pain,
Its pleasure,
Leave no path untaken.
Neil Gaiman, The Grave yard Book
The fates lead him who will;
him who won't they drag.
Joseph Campbell, The Power of Myth

As I have shared before, I suffered from chronic back pain for ten years, that neither Western nor Chinese medicine seemed to be able to resolve for more than a short time. Then, during the summer of 1996 while I was teaching a graduate continuing studies class at Hamline University, a student noticed that I was moving gingerly, as one does with back pain, and approached me privately after class. Pei-Ju was from China and in St. Paul teaching Mandarin Chinese. She decided to take a couple of graduate classes at Hamline, which turned out to be lucky, or as I now think, synchronistic, for me. She told me about a qigong master from China who had healed her injured back and was now living in Los Angeles. She would be willing to contact him and ask if he would be willing to see me. I thanked Pei-Ju and told her I would think about it. When I got home, I told Wendy about this and she urged me to have Pei-Ju contact him. I also spoke with

Master Mark who went to his altar to consult the spirits who told him that I should go. At our next class, I told Pei-Ju I would appreciate her contacting this qigong master, whose name was Hong Liu.

I spent the rest of the summer, autumn, and the Christmas holidays procrastinating and debating with myself as to whether I should spend money to fly to LA and stay in a hotel for a week for a treatment that probably would not work any better than the others I had tried. But after some encouraging and coaxing from Wendy, I finally made an appointment to see Hong Liu in April, during the school district's spring break. In the meantime, I searched the internet for information about Hong Liu, and discovered that in addition to being a qigong master, he was a medical doctor who trained in Western medicine in Shanghai. He had also written a book, :*Mastering Miracles: The healing Art of Qigong as Taught by a Master* that had just been published that winter. I purchased his book, and as I read his story, I became guardedly excited about my upcoming visit. Now, you have to understand that being "guardedly excited" is a common reaction for me. Maybe it is because I am an introvert, or maybe because I had lived amongst the upper mid-western Scandinavian Lutherans for so long, but Wendy would tell you that this is indeed my common reaction to something new: Don't get too excited in case it doesn't turn out as well as I hoped.

Spring break finally arrived and I flew to Los Angeles. I drove my rental car to a hotel near Hong Liu's house. The hotel was undergoing some renovations but it had a nice garden in back with white roses blooming. It was a lovely place where I practiced my morning qigong during my stay. As soon as I entered my room and set my suitcase on the bed, I noticed a basket of flowers on the table. Reading the attached card, I saw that it was from Wendy. It was a very romantic gesture as I was already missing her. I immediately called to thank her and tell her that I had arrived safely and to share how the bright flowers had lifted my spirits. As I unpacked,

I also saw a little bundle of greeting cards in envelopes tied together with a ribbon and a smile spread across my face. You see, we had established a practice that whenever we are apart, we would leave an I Miss You or I Love You card for each night of our separation. Opening these cards always makes me happy, and gives me something tangible from my lover to touch when we are apart. I usually read my card just before turning out the lights, hoping it will induce good dreams.

After unpacking and settling in, I rested for a while in my hotel room until it was time to drive to Master Hong's for my late afternoon appointment. Once I arrived in his neighborhood it was easy to find his house because of the big gate with a black and white yin yang symbol on it. I buzzed at the gate. Once my appointment was verified, the gate slid open and I drove through and parked in a designated area under an arbor that somewhat protected the parked cars from the scorching California sun. As I got out of my car, I was greeted by four barking dogs, whose wagging tails let me know they were friendly. They escorted me to the front door of the house where I was greeted by one of Master Hong's apprentices, Lynn, who showed me to a seat, handed me a clipboard, and told me to fill out the top of the form attached. She then returned to teaching a woman a qigong exercise. I wrote my name in English and in Chinese, and my birthdate and time of birth on the form. On the rest of the page were two outlines of a human body, a front and back view. It was similar to those I had filled out many times for physical therapists and chiropractors. At those venues, I had always been asked to mark my areas of pain on the drawings. But curiously, Lynn told me not to mark on this body outline at all, which seemed rather odd.

Behind a wooden Chinese screen, I could partially hear and see Hong Liu and his interpreter. An elderly gentleman was talking about his cancer. When they were finished, Hong Liu walked him into the room where I was waiting and told Lynn to teach him some specific qigong exercises. Then

Master Hong walked over to me, took the paper and clipboard from me, and smiling, motioned for me to follow him. I sat down nervously in the chair he pointed to behind the screen. He sat across from me, and looking at my name, asked through his interpreter, how to pronounce it. Then he asked about my Chinese name. I told him it had been given to me by my kung fu and qigong teacher, Master Mark. He asked a few questions about Master Mark, that I answered and then kept nervously chattering on. He put his finger to his lips and said, "relax." Then taking a deep breath and exhaling, he looked at me intently, occasionally marking on the figures on the paper I gave him with a red pen. He then got up and poured a cup of steaming hot green tea into a paper cup and pointed his fingers down toward the tea from above. He said through his interpreter that he was charging the tea with qi. Then, handing the paper cup to me, he directed me to drink all of it but to be careful because it was very hot. He said that I should relax and pay attention to where in my body I felt the energy of the tea. I sipped it as quickly as I could without burning my tongue and tried to relax and feel the energy. I could feel the heat from the hot liquid in my stomach as expected, but then I began to feel warmth going down my injured back and down my legs. I could also feel heat in my upper shoulders, neck, and in the back of my head. Then I began to feel heat behind my eyes causing them to water. I reported this to Master Hong and he smiled nodding his head in affirmation.

Standing up, Master Hong motioned for me to follow him into his adjacent treatment room. In the center of the room was a massage table on which he told me to lie face down. He began the treatment that was a combination of energy work and acupressure. Even when his hands were six to eight inches above my body while he did the energy work, it felt as if he were actually touching me. The feeling was so strong, that if someone would have asked whether he was touching me or not, I would have bet money that he was. Sometimes he would stop and apply strong acupressure to certain spots.

## Chapter Seven: The Paths Begin to Converge

When he applied this pressure to some points, it was somewhat painful. When I winced, he would say, "Yes, energy blocked here." I had never felt anything like this energy before. It was strong and palpable and made me sleepy and lightheaded, and yet paradoxically, energized. He then directed me to turn over and lie on my back and continued the treatment. Finally, he had me stand, and placing one hand above my head and another on my low back, continued his energy work. I felt like a marionette under his control, my body swaying and following his hand without any direction from my brain. When he was finished, he directed me back to the area where we first sat and he began to talk to me through his interpreter again.

He showed me the form on which he had marked on the figure. There were red marks on the low back on the right side, the right knee, the upper back, shoulders and back of the neck. He also had a mark across the chest, across the eyes, and on the left ankle. He began by saying he could see I had injured my left ankle a few times but that it had healed nicely. This was true. I first sprained my ankle during high school football and again twice playing pickup basketball with friends. He said my back injury was from an accident or trauma, and as you already know, that was also correct. Then he commented that there was something wrong with my eyes, maybe glaucoma, which was also true. I had been diagnosed with a rare glaucoma a couple of years earlier. He then said I had injured my neck many years ago and I still got headaches from this. Again true. I was in a bad automobile accident during my freshman year of college, and my neck had given me headaches ever since. Then he said I had a heart problem. I was surprised and responded that I didn't have any heart problems. My cholesterol levels and blood pressure were normal. He ignored my contradiction and then said my back and neck were not a big problem and that he thought he could correct these before I went home and if I continue to do the qigong exercises, he prescribed, I could control it. My eyes were more troublesome, he told me, and he didn't know how effective his work would be in this area. He was most concerned, he said, about my heart and was worried that if I didn't correct it, I would have a heart attack eventually. He said he thought this heart problem was genetic, but he would teach me qigong exercises that would help. It turns out he was right about that also. In May, of 2019, I had urgent open-heart surgery and a double coronary bypass. The heart surgeon at Mayo Clinic said this was a genetic problem, just as Master Hong had pronounced twenty-two years earlier. Later, as Master Hong's student, I asked how he could know these things. He explained that he can see where the qi is blocked or effected by some previous injuries or illness and may cause a future problem. Because of his dual education in both Western and Chinese Medicine, he was able to talk about problems from both perspectives. This is something I would eventually be able to do later when teaching qigong in a hospital or clinic setting.

During the rest of that week, I was treated by Master Hong three more times. He prescribed specific qigong exercises and directed Lynn to teach them to me. Master Hong also said that I should continue to practice Master Mark's Six Sounds Qigong, after asking me to show him some of the qigong exercises and my kung fu. In addition to continuing the prescribed qigong exercises twice daily, Master Hong also said I should eat a vegetarian diet for what turned out to be about nine months, and then I could slowly add back small amounts of meat. He gave me the names of a couple of local restaurants that would accommodate the kind of vegetarian diet he wanted me to eat while I was in LA. I tried a Chinese restaurant and an Egyptian restaurant on his list and they were both very good. Since I was going to be in Los Angeles for a week, I asked Master Hong if there was a qigong class I could attend while I was there. He said he wasn't teaching any classes then, but he would arrange for one of his apprentices to teach me. Lynn, who had already taught me his prescribed exercises, met with me for three full days, teaching me Master Hong's Awakening Healing Energy Qigong exercises. In addition, she shared information about the

Chinese Five Elements or Five Phase Theory, as well as some of Master Hong's qigong diagnosis and treatment methods.

Something else happened during that first visit with Hong Liu that significantly and positively influenced my hero's journey. While I was in Los Angeles, I read Kenneth Cohen's book, *The Way of Qigong: The Art and Science of Chinese Energy Healing*. In it, Cohen made the following comment: "Perhaps China and the West can begin to harvest the best of both worlds. We can combine the energy medicine technology of qigong with the insights and methodology of psychotherapy to create a new and truly effective system of mind-body healing." This comment, as well as Hong Liu's emphasis on the importance of using both qigong and Western Medicine, engendered in me, an aspiration to combine psychotherapy and qigong in my own counseling work. Synchronistically, Lynn was also a psychotherapist, and was excited to discuss this idea during our time together. We shared how we might implement this with some of the individuals with whom we were currently working. Years later, this integrated approach, that had its beginnings in my pondering on a comment by Ken Cohen, and in discussions with Lynn, would be expanded and fully developed as my doctoral dissertation, titled *An Integrative Approach to Transpersonal Counseling*.

By the end of my week in Los Angeles, my back pain was almost completely gone. On my last day with Lynn and Master Hong, I brought flowers and placed them on the table in his waiting area, next to the Kuan Yin statue that was on it. Before giving me a last qigong treatment, Master Hong thanked me for the flowers and then motioned for me to follow him outside where he tested me on the exercises Lynn had taught me during the week. After completing all of the exercises, he told me to do the lung exercise again, saying, "This time I will do it with you and share my energy." As we did the exercise together, I could feel tingling in my fingers and he said, "You feel qi in your fingers." Next, we did the heart exercise together and I could feel energy like I never have before in my hands and chest. He then told me to look at my palms and they were very red. He showed me his palms and they were also red. He told me that if I practice consistently and conscientiously, I would eventually feel the energy just like I experienced it now, doing it with him. He was right. This did happen after several years of regular and dedicated practice.

Before I left, Master Hong also gave me a brown paper lunch bag filled with a variety of herbs, bark, and something that looked suspiciously like a snake skin. He directed me to make a tea from this and drink a cup twice daily until it was gone. The day after I arrived home, Wendy made a big pot of it, following the written directions carefully. The house smelled very bad. When I took my first sip, my gag reflex was triggered, making it difficult to swallow it. Master Hong warned me that this might happen, and said I could add a teaspoon of local honey to each cup to help temper the flavor. Adding honey helped, but it still would not be my choice for tea time. After pouring the tea into mason jars, there remained a thick layer of sludge on the bottom of the pot. Wendy, being the artist that she is, took some of this remaining muck and sculpted it into a small animal similar to a Southwest Native American fetish and placed it on a book shelf in my home office. Within a week of being home and regularly practicing the qigong exercises Master Hong prescribed, my back pain was completely gone. I worried that like in the past with other interventions, the pain would return after some amount of time. But over the years, as long as I maintain a regular qigong practice, I am free of back pain and I very rarely have a headache. If my back pain returns because I've shoveled heavy snow or worked too hard in the yard or gardens, I return to the prescribed exercises and the pain is resolved within a few days.

I continued to meet with Hong Liu as both a patient and a student, flying to Los Angeles or Phoenix, where he also did workshops, a couple of times a year for the next nine years. Master Hong had become another

## Chapter Seven: The Paths Begin to Converge

important mentor on my hero's journey. After Master Mark gave me my teaching certificate, I took all the four levels of Hong Liu's classes and learned qigong exercises and interventions for various health problems privately. My external qigong healing ability, or using my own qi to help relieve pain and open blocked energy channels in others, improved quite a bit. Eventually, Master Hong allowed me to assist with some of his classes. I would see him privately first on Friday for a qigong treatment, and to ask him questions about how to heal others. Then, I would help teach prescribed exercises to people who came for a healing session. Then, on Saturday and Sunday, I was assigned to help one of the small groups with the Basic Qigong Exercises they were learning in Class. On Friday and Saturday evenings, Master Hong worked with his advanced students, which he now considered me to be. I still see Hong Liu occasionally. Wendy and I both saw him in Hawaii in February of 2020. I had a paralyzed right diaphragm muscle and lung as a result of my open-heart surgery. Within a day after being treated by Master Hong, my diaphragm muscle and lung began to slowly function again. By mid-summer, my lung doctor said that my latest tests showed my pulmonary capacity was again in the normal range. She was very curious about what Master Hong had done.

Joseph Campbell tells us, that the hero's journey is only complete once the hero shares what they have learned with others in the community. The road to sharing, however, was not a straight or an easy one for me. While the idea was appealing, it would take an unrelenting series of events to nudge me, or should I say, push me, to share what I had learned beyond family, a few close friends, and students. A powerful dream was the prelude to a new road of trials that prodded me towards sharing my new skills with a more far-reaching group of people. As I was drifting off to sleep one night, I was praying that I would get information in my dream that would help me on my journey. I kept saying, *show me what I should do*. After falling asleep, I had the following dream. Wendy and I are at a waterfall. It is not very high but wide and strong. We go swimming in the water below the falls and it feels very refreshing, although sometimes, I feel frightened because the power of the current is quite strong, and I worry that it might sweep us away. A group of protestors are on the shore. They want to dam up the river above the falls to control it. They said it would be safer then. Suddenly, a person I had met in waking life, arrives at the scene. At the time, he was a college professor, but also described himself as a spiritual healer. From the first time I saw him in waking life and read some of his work, he really brought out the Mr. Carson in me. While I admired him for his intelligence, academic credentials, and unique cultural experiences, he did not exhibit the persona, nor behave in the proper manner for a college professor. He is in many ways, my antithesis. While I am an introvert, he is an extrovert whose healing technique involves moving around freely, almost dancing, and making vocal sounds. I tend to downplay my own knowledge and skills, while he lauds himself, and has been accused of exaggerating his claims. What he does exemplify however, and I needed, is his willingness to act freely without fear. In the dream, he asks Wendy and me to protest with him to keep the dam from being built so that the waterfall can remain free. Now, maybe because of my introverted personality, I do not join in on protest marches or gatherings, even when it is for a good cause. The location of my dream shifts, and I am now in my therapy office at the Scott County Mental Health Center. I am counseling a person and holding a small bottle of Chinese medicinal oil that Master Mark had given to me in awake life. I begin to rub some of the oil on the person's temples, telling them that it will help to reduce their stress. I then anoint the person, like a priest does, with the sign of the cross (a foreshadowing). At that point, in my dream, I begin to feel anxiety and I worry that

## Chapter Seven: The Paths Begin to Converge

I will get into trouble and lose my job. All of a sudden, this same professor appears somehow in the office, and assures me that what I am doing is very good. The dream ends.

Reflecting on this dream, the waterfall and powerful current below it seems to be archetypal images for qi. Part of me wanted to let it flow through me, to feel its power, and make use of it in my healing work, but some other aspect of my psyche wanted to control it, to dam it up, because it is scary and it is not an accepted part of psychotherapy. Although both Master Mark and Master Hong sometime used oils during qigong treatments, psychotherapists do not use healing oils, nor do they anoint people. The professor in my dream was that aspect of my shadow that wanted to break free from the norm and convention, and incorporate qigong into my psychotherapy practice.

Biddings to combine psychotherapy and qigong came more insistently through a series of synchronistic events that happened shortly after this dream. It began with Wendy and I being invited as guest lecturers at the University of Aukland in New Zealand. We taught a class on Conflict Resolution which incorporated the concept of accept, blend, and redirect that we had adapted from our Peaceful Warrior Intensive. After our class was finished at the University, we stayed on for a ten-day holiday, traveling around and visiting various places on New Zealand's North Island. One evening, in Rotorua, we attended a traditional Maori cultural performance, preceded by a lovely dinner. At our table was a woman from Rarotonga with her children, a young exchange student from Germany, and a couple from San Francisco. After dinner, the show began and the singing and dancing was wonderful. At one point, one of the performers asked that one person at each table volunteer to come up on stage later during the show. The exchange student at our table volunteered, and that was agreeable to everyone else.

However, when one of the women performers came to our table to escort our volunteer on stage, she informed me that I also needed to come with her. I politely protested, explaining that we already had a volunteer from our table. Now, as I mentioned before, I am an introvert. This may seem strange to some of you who have seen me presenting to groups of a couple of hundred people, or heard me preach at a church, or to those who are aware of the little known fact that I played electric bass in a rock band in high school and on stage in college. But all of those experiences are okay for an introvert. In those situations, I am up on the stage, or at the podium or pulpit that is separated from the large group in clearly defined ways. Most of all, I am well prepared and feel in control of the situation. But in this situation, when the Maori woman persisted, and took me by the hand, escorting me up to the stage, I was not in control, nor was I at all prepared for what was to come.

Once on stage, the volunteers and I joined the performers in a traditional poi dance. This involved swinging two fiber balls, about the size of tennis balls on the end of pieces of rope about two feet long, one in each hand, rhythmically to the music in various patterns. After trying to do this and smacking my body and head with the poi ball several times, the music mercifully ended. But we were not done yet. To my dismay, the Maori men then challenged the male recruits to join them in a Hakka, the traditional men's dance to show strength and courage. I still delude myself into thinking that I didn't look too bad doing this, and mercifully, Wendy did not take any videos, so I remain safe in my delusion. In any case, it was very uncomfortable and embarrassing.

After leaving New Zealand, we extended our vacation for a few more days on beautiful Rarotonga in the Cook Islands. On one of our days there, we joined a small group on a boat that took us snorkeling out on the reef. After a beautiful time snorkeling, the crew took us to one of the small outlying islands and cooked a fantastic grilled picnic lunch. When we finished our meal, one of the muscular young men demonstrated how the Islanders climb a tree to get a coconut, and then bringing one back, talked about the coconut's many uses in Polynesian culture. Later, Wendy volunteered to be a model while one of the young men demonstrated how the Island women wear the traditional Polynesian cloth, called a *pareo*. I was so glad she was volunteering this time. But then, she asked the young man, "How do the men wear this?" One of the crew members looked at me and said with a smile, "Do you know what your wife just did to you sir?" So again, I had to stand in front of our small group and be the model for the men's version of wearing the pareo that to Western eyes, looks somewhat like wearing a big colorful diaper. First, I was asked to take off my shirt, which I just don't do unless I'm swimming. On a positive note, Wendy was laughing so hard that she was unable to take any photos. Again, after I was in the local island attire, I was asked to join with two of the young men in another Hakka. Returning home after our stay on Rarotonga, felt good. I stayed in Los Angeles for a couple of days to work with Master Hong, while Wendy continued back to Wisconsin, where we now lived in a small river town, just across from Minnesota where we still worked.

A month later, on our wedding anniversary, Wendy and I decided to celebrate with a romantic dinner at the Bali Hai Supper Club in St. Paul. We hoped it would remind us of our visit to Rarotonga. After dinner, there was a show with Polynesian music and dancers and because it was our anniversary, we were called up on stage with another couple celebrating their special event, to dance a hula with the performers. It was embarrassing, but at least this time, Wendy was on stage with me.

During that following winter, Wendy and I purchased tickets to see an African dance troop performance at the Ordway Theater in St. Paul. During the intermission several of the dancers set up a cordoned off circle in the lobby area and kept it free of people except a few of the dancers. Once the area was set up, they called for volunteers to join them dancing in their makeshift circle. This time I was having none of it, so as soon as they called for volunteers, I stealthily slipped away and hid behind a pillar in the lobby away from the performers, where I could still see them, but was sure they couldn't see me. The drumming and dancing started and they were joined in the circle by several young African American children and a couple of African American women. As they were dancing, one of the male dancers left the circle, walked right over to where I was hiding, smiled at me, and gestured for me to come with him. When I shook my head no, he gently took me by the arm and led me to the dance circle. I was the only man in the circle except for the male performers and the only white person in the group, so of course, I stuck out like a proverbial sore thumb. This dancing thing was getting too strange to believe. Now if you haven't seen traditional African dance, I will tell you that they move their shoulders in ways mine just did not want to move and there were leaps and jumps that I was not accustomed to doing, ever.

On the way home, as I was complaining about my being called to dance again, Wendy shared her thoughts with me. She pointed out, that what all of these indigenous dancers from various cultures had in common, was that they really surrendered to the dance. It seemed to her that the Divine Guide was trying to tell me to surrender to the dance, and to be willing to use my qigong with people in my counseling work, not just with family and friends. I, while deep down acknowledging the wisdom of her words, wanted to believe that these dance incidents were just coincidences.

The following year, we were invited again to be guest teachers at the University of Auckland. On the Saturday before our class began, we decided to visit the Auckland Cultural Museum. We arrived about ten minutes before the Maori Cultural Show began, so we bought tickets and this time, as we entered the auditorium, I insisted on sitting in the back row where it was darkest. The show began with the women singing a song and swinging poi balls in intricate patterns to the music. When the opening dance ended, one of the women asked for volunteers to join them on stage. I immediately felt my body tense up and I'm sure I had sunk down in my seat a bit, trying to be invisible. A couple of people from the audience got up and joined the performers on stage, and the Maori woman who seemed to be in charge of the group, explained what they were going to do. The music started, and a sense of relief flooded through me. But then, after less than a minute, the leader said, "Stop the music." Without saying anything else, she came down from the stage, walked all the way up the center aisle to the back of the auditorium and right up to where we were sitting. She looked at me and said, "You come too." I was dumbfounded. Wendy, because of her extraverted nature, and perhaps taking pity on me, said she would love to come instead. But the woman was insistent, saying, "We need him." In a daze and thinking, how could this possibly be happening again, she took me by the hand and led me up to the stage where I again proceeded to make a fool of myself, trying to do a poi dance, and thumping myself in the head with the poi balls a few times. As unbelievable as it may seem, my ordeal wasn't over yet. After leaving New Zealand, we spent ten days vacationing in Australia. At the Tjapukai's Aboriginal Cultural Centre, while sitting about midway up in the bleachers, I was again picked out of the crowd to dance with the men. This time dancing while imitating various animals. I remember having to jump around like a kangaroo and mimic a soaring bird.

Perhaps you have seen the meme on Facebook that claims to be a Zen proverb. It reads, "Let go or be dragged." Maybe Wendy was right. Maybe the Spirit was trying to tell me something, and because I wasn't listening, I was being dragged. Then, the clincher occurred shortly after returning home from our trip to New Zealand and Australia. While browsing in a local book store, a book title caught my eye because of its synchronistic title. It was *The Dancing Healers* by Carl Hammerschlag. I just had to purchase this book and I began reading it as soon as we got home. Dr.

Hammerschlag, who had worked at a hospital serving the Pueblo people of the Southwestern United States, wrote about how his work there changed his medical and psychiatric practice, and his life. The book begins with a story that was another synchronicity. It tells about an encounter Dr. Hammerschlag had with Santiago, a Pueblo clan chief and priest, who had been admitted to the hospital with congestive heart failure. When Dr. Hammerschlag entered the old man's room to examine him, the chief asked with a serene smile, "Where did you learn to heal?" Hammerschlag described his encounter like this:

> I responded almost by rote, rattling off my medical education, internship, and certification. Again, the beatific smile and another question: "Do you know how to dance?" Somehow touched by whimsy at the old man's query, I answered that, sure, I liked to dance; and I shuffled a little at his bedside. Santiago chuckled, got out of bed, and, short of breath, began to show me his dance. "You must be able to dance if you are to heal people," he said. "And will you teach me your steps?" I asked, indulging the aging priest. Santiago nodded. "Yes, I can teach you my steps, but you will have to hear your own music. (10)

My experiences of being called to dance with indigenous people, and then finding and reading this account in Hammerschlag's book, had a powerful impact on me and I found my eyes filling with tears. Wendy again proposed that being called to dance meant overcoming my fear of working with others as a qigong healer as well as a psychotherapist. She added that I needed to surrender to the dance and even be willing to make a fool of myself and fail if necessary. I was being called to do as writer Anne LaMott wrote in her book *Bird by Bird: Some Instructions on Writing and Life*, "Don't look at your feet to see if you are doing it right. Just dance." I had been so worried about doing qigong "right" or seeming weird, or failing, that I was afraid to just surrender to the qi of the universe and metaphorically dance with my counselees. The Chinese character (zi), is used as a title meaning "master" such as in the founder of Taoism, Laozi (Old Master). But the character also means "child," and (zi) actually depicts a dancing child. This brings me back to my many dancing synchronicities, and to what Jesus taught: Unless we become like children, we will never enter the realm of heaven (Matt 18:3). Jelaluddin Rumi said it this way, "Whoever knows the power of the dance dwells in God" (qtd in Pascal 185). Years later, in seminary, I would learn that some of the earliest Christian theologians referred to the Holy Trinity as the great *Perichoresis*, or circle dance, in which we are all invited to join.

Once I was able to accept the meaning behind these synchronistic dancing events, I wrote a proposal for integrating psychotherapy and clinical hypnosis with qigong therapy. I sent it to Master Hong for his input and asked him if he would write a letter of endorsement. He said that he liked the proposal but that Lynn should write the letter because she was a psychologist and she and I had conversations regarding how we could integrate qigong and psychotherapy with individuals. She agreed to write the letter. I submitted the proposal, along with Lynn's letter, to the HealthEast Care System, where I was already teaching qigong classes to staff in a couple of different locations. My proposal was accepted and I was approved to implement this integrative approach at HealthEast's Healing Center, where I was already teaching a qigong class. The only thing left to do was to talk with the Minnesota Board of Psychology and get their approval. One concern was that the rules were very clear that psychologists were not allowed to touch their patients, and the qigong that I had learned, sometimes involved acupressure. The medical director of the Healing Center and I met with a member of the board of psychology, and after explaining the proposal, it was approved with the requirement that counselees be given a handout clarifying the distinction between psychotherapy and qigong, and sign a form agreeing to appropriate touch in the context of the qigong therapy if they so desired. An offhanded comment by the board member as we were leaving, inadvertently contributed to the next stage of my hero's journey. She said that it was too bad I wasn't a minister, because ministers traditionally use the laying on of hands in prayer, and the board doesn't interfere because of separation of church and state issues.

It wasn't long before I began using this new approach with two individuals who were in my qigong class at the Healing Center. Both were dealing with chronic illnesses and pain, and both were very interested in experiencing qigong therapy along with traditional psychotherapy as a new approach to helping them find some relief from their pain and sorting out the emotional issues that are inevitable when one has ongoing pain and illness. I still run into one of these individuals out in the community once in a while. She continues to practice qigong and tells me how glad she was to try something new that helped relieve her pain and gave her a sense of control over her illness.

Since I submitted that proposal, I have never been called up to dance at a performance of indigenous people again. Dance however, did continue to play a role in Wendy's and my life. For Wendy's birthday one year I gave her the present of a series of ballroom dance lessons. We enjoyed it so much that we took dance classes for several years. We learned some ballroom, swing, and salsa and met other couples in dance class with whom we are still friends. I have even led a retreat titled, *The Spirituality of the Dance*.

The Natural Healing Center closed its doors about a year after I started the integrative counseling work there, when HealthEast's Woodwinds Hospital opened in Woodbury Minnesota. Woodwinds was founded with the philosophy that traditional Western and alternative therapies could coexist, resulting in more effective holistic healing. I was asked to teach qigong there, and allowed to continue my work with individuals using integrative therapy. Woodwinds conducted studies on the efficacy of alternative therapies: acupuncture, energy based therapies such as Healing Touch and qigong, the use of essential oils, and massage. The results consistently demonstrated that these modalities are indeed helpful to the patients who use them.

In the course of our life, most of us have experienced some type of coincidence in which two or more seemingly independent events, that have no apparent logical or causal connection, have a meaningful linkage. Richard Tarnas, the founding director of the graduate program in Philosophy, Cosmology and Consciousness at the California Institute of Integral Studies, writing about these coincidences said, "The patterning can strike one as so extraordinary that it is difficult to believe the coincidence has been produced by chance alone. The events give the distinct impression of having been precisely arranged, invisibly orchestrated" (Cosmos and Psyche). This is how it seemed with the dancing "coincidences." It was as if there were just too many to be coincidental. Carl Jung was so fascinated by these events that he began calling them synchronicity. He referred to this force that lures us to completeness or individuation, as the Holy Spirit, although he remained agnostic regarding the source of this "Holy Spirit." He could not be sure whether it was somehow innately built into the unconscious, or whether it was some independent cosmic force trying to bring us into some kind of quantum harmony. Catholic deacon, pastoral minister, and author, Lex Ferrauiola has no doubts of the source of synchronicity. He is convinced that these events are the result of the Holy Spirit, the Divine Energies sending us a message, albeit in code, at some crossroads in life, when we are experiencing tentativeness and uncertainty.

# Chapter Eight

# *The Way of the Shen Fu*

*Our inner guidance comes to us through our feelings and body wisdom first, not through intellectual understanding. The intellect works best in service to our intuition,
our inner guidance, soul, God or higher power, whichever term we choose for the spiritual energy that animates life.*
Christiane Northrup, MD, Goddesses Never Age

It was Master Mark's birthday and I had tried to find a certain incense he liked to burn at his altar in the Asian stores around town with no luck. Then after work, as Wendy and I were driving down University Avenue in St. Paul, we saw a little Asian grocery store, complete with roasted ducks hanging by their feet in the window. We stopped there and after perusing the aisles a bit, we found the incense we were looking for. We took three boxes and then looked at the variety of joss paper, thinking we could use it for wrapping paper. We found a nice piece that worked well. On it were drawings of fish and flowers and a section with a design enclosing Chinese writing. In the car, Wendy wrapped the incense and a gift certificate from one of Sifu's favorite restaurants and then we drove to the kung fu school to give him his present.

When we arrived, there were only a few students at class and one of the advanced students was teaching them, so Master Mark was free. We gave him the wrapped present and a birthday card and wished him a happy birthday. The section of paper with the Chinese writing was centered on top of the package as we handed it to him. His eyes lit up. He said that the writing was very special and that he had been waiting for someone to bring it to him, or something to that effect. He then carefully took the paper off the present trying not to tear it. He set down the incense saying that it was the right kind, and that the spirits like it. Then he went back to examining the joss paper. I told him that there was something else inside, so after finding the gift certificate and thanking us, he again was drawn back to the joss paper. Folding it carefully, so that only the writing was showing, he told us it was a very special prayer to Kuan Yin, the goddess or bodhisattva of compassion. He said we should take it home, cut out the section with the prayer and put it under the incense pot on our home altar. I said, "No Sifu, it's for you." He responded sharply, "No, you do what I say." Then, with the joss paper in hand, he told me to follow him to the school altar where he began to chant the words on the paper, that began with *Namo Kuan Shi Yin Pusa*. He told me to chant along the best I could. It was one of my favorite memories of Master Mark. When we finished chanting, Sifu told me to come back the next day and he would translate the chant into English for me to write down. Then he told me that I was ready to learn *shengong*. Now shengong was a term I had heard Sifu use before, but didn't really understand what it meant at the time.

Let me explain. The qigong I was studying is a method for working with qi, which literally means "air" or "breath" but also means "life force" or "vital energy." These descriptions do not fully explain the depth and complexity of the concept of qi in Chinese philosophy. Qi is similar to the *pneuma* of Greek Stoic philosophy, *prana* in Indian philosophy, and *ruach* in Hebrew and Judaism. It is the field of energy that orders and harmonizes the universe. It surrounds, permeates, and vitalizes all matter. Qi influences the weather, moves the planets and the galaxies along their orbits, and energizes all of life. Qi guides the patterns of the seasons and the process of evolution. It seems pretty obvious that George Lucas got his idea for the Force in Star Wars from the concept of qi. Obi-Wan Kenobi tells young Luke Skywalker, that the Force "surrounds us, penetrates us, and

## Chapter Eight: The Way of the Shen Fu

binds the galaxy together." Yoda expands this teaching, telling Luke, "You must feel the Force around you, here, between you, me, the tree, the rock, everywhere." The Chinese character *gong* used in qigong means working to develop a skill, or cultivating as one cultivates a garden. Through qigong exercises, students learn to use their qi to strengthen their immune system and enhance healing in themselves or others.

*Shen* on the other hand, means spirit. It can refer to spiritual beings such as the bodhisattvas, gods, or other spirit helpers. In our Western spiritual traditions, the shen could be thought of as angels or saints. But like qi, shen also has additional meanings. It can refer to the human mind or psyche, the soul, and in its purest form, divine light. It is, to borrow from Pope Francis, "A spark of divine light is within each of us."

Shengong therefore, means spirit work. Just as people can learn to cultivate and move their bodily qi and the qi of others, they can also learn to mentally tune into and be guided by the divine light within, as well as to be sensitive to the unseen world and become more effective at following spiritual guidance. In the Western Christian tradition in which I grew up, it was common to pray to the Blessed Mother, or to the saints or our guardian angel, to intercede with God on our behalf. Many of my protestant friends misunderstand this. They confuse prayer with worship. Praying to the saints is prayer in the sense of its Old English usage, "Pray tell, or "pray sit." To pray under this definition simply means to request or entreat, to ask for help.

When I spoke with Master Mark alone the following day, he told me that if I wanted to learn shengong, I would have to come to his altar for 39 consecutive days. He explained that this number was significant because the number 3 sounds like the Chinese word for life or giving birth and the number 9 is 3 times 3 and signifies the spiritual doorway through which we connect with the unseen world. Each day, he continued, I would have to light a stick of incense, then stand in horseback riding stance holding the incense in prayer hands in front of his altar until the incense burned itself out. This turned out to be harder than I first imagined. Each incense stick burned for about forty-five minutes. Furthermore, if I missed a day, I had to start the 39 days all over again. Explaining further, he told me I should be meditating during this time and thinking about what kind of help I want from the spirits. I would soon find out that it was very difficult to meditate when your legs and arms are shaking and burning with pain from standing in horse stance that long. If I was worthy, he told me, spirit helpers would reveal themselves to me. Sifu then touched my shoulder and said, "I know the spirits will pick you." After the meditation at the altar each day, Sifu would teach me specific methods for using shengong to help myself and others.

During the time I was learning shengong I had the following dream: I am putting on an alb, a cincture, and stole in the sacristy of a church that seems Roman Catholic or Episcopalian. I think to my dream self, *I shouldn't be wearing vestments because I'm not a priest*. I walk out to the altar and bow to it. Then I turn and walk down towards the congregation. I see Wendy sitting in the first row next to the center aisle. As I walk past her, I smile—and touch her hand. I then start to give a sermon, beginning by singing the first verse of *Amazing Grace: Amazing grace, how sweet the sound that saved a wretch like me. I once was lost but now am found, was blind but now I see*. This strange dream would prove prophetic and I would discover later, that the Chinese title for a Christian priest is *shenfu*, meaning spirit father.

The first setback in my shengong training occurred only a couple of weeks into my daily training. I had to teach a late workshop and skipped a day at Sifu's altar. When I arrived the following day, he asked why I missed the day before. Then he told me I would have to start my 39 days all over again. I guess I hadn't taken this warning literally when we started, so I was somewhat surprised. I didn't miss another day after that. On day thirty-one of

## Chapter Eight: The Way of the Shen Fu

my new start at Sifu's altar, I was getting frustrated. Nothing seemed to be happening. I kept thinking, *I don't think there are any spirits here. If there are any spirits, why don't you show yourself.* Then while I was meditating with my eyes closed, vivid, colorful images passed in front of my eyelids like on a movie screen. First, Chinese writing in bright yellow formed on the dark background of my closed eyelids and then disappeared. Then, a Chinese opera style mask came from the right side of my vision, stopped briefly in front of my face, and then moved on. Several other masks did the same thing. Finally, a large eagle came flying at me from the altar and pushed me backwards. It seemed so real, that I could feel its talons touching my chest and pushing me. It was so powerful that I actually stumbled backwards and fell to the floor. As I laid on the floor, I felt dizzy and a tingling in my fingers, hands, legs, head, and chest. Master Mark quickly came over and asked what happened. When I told him, he informed me that one of the spirits with whom he works at the altar is Golden Eagle, and I had insulted it by saying I didn't think there were spirits. He got a chair and told me to sit down. Now, he said, I had to light a new incense stick, apologize to the spirits, and start over for the day. After I finished the meditation, he told me that he also sometimes sees symbols similar to Chinese writing that he doesn't understand. The masks, he said were different spirits checking me out. A few days after this event, for three mornings in a row, in my half-asleep, half-awake state, I saw a distinct Chinese character. On the last morning, I drew it on a piece of paper, as best I could remember it, and that afternoon I showed it to Sifu. He said it was *Ling*, meaning spirit power. This image was good, he informed me, as it meant the spirits wanted to work with me. Ling literally refers to a person who works between heaven and earth and can call upon spiritual energy. He drew the character on yellow paper and told me to also place it under the incense pot on our home altar.

One Saturday morning, as we arrived for qigong class, Wendy had a sore neck and shoulder. She had been to a chiropractor but got little relief. Sifu told me to light incense at the altar and pray for her and use a shengong formula he had taught me. I made a certain symbol on a piece of plain yellow joss paper and then burned it at the altar. Then I mixed the ashes from the paper with some *dit da jow* (lineament) that Sifu makes and rubbed it into her shoulder and neck saying to myself, "I put this on and the pain is gone," while rubbing it in. When I was finished, Wendy said that the pain was gone. This is one simple example of shengong healing.

September 11, 1999 was a very special day for me. I received my teaching certificate from Master Mark with a traditional Chinese ceremony. Every day of the prior week, I spent time with Sifu so he could prepare me. I had to bring three boxes of incense, two red candles, joss paper, fruit, flowers, tea for the altar and a bottle of Chinese brandy (baijiu). Additionally, I brought a red card in which I wrote my name, the date and time of my birth, and my intention to be a good teacher and healer. Sifu's altar is pretty crowded. On the center of the wall behind it was a large framed red piece of paper with black Chinese calligraphy from his teacher. To the left of that, another large red paper with black Taoist symbols, some similar to the ones I had learned in shengong. Below that on the altar was a large bronze statue of the Medicine Buddha. In the center of the altar were the Chinese gods of luck, prosperity, and long life. These three are often seen on small altars in Chinese restaurants. Other statues on the altar were Kuan Yin, goddess of compassion, and Kuan Gong, god of martial arts, Da Mo, who brought Buddhism to China and founded the Shaolin temple, and a statue of Zhong Guei, the demon and evil ghost vanquisher. Sifu's spirit fan was also on the altar. I had the spirit fan that I made as part of my shengong training on his altar too. In front of the statues were three brass incense burners, and three cups of tea in front of those. There were also small empty cups. On either side of the altar were the traditional Fu Dogs to protect the altar.

## Chapter Eight: The Way of the Shen Fu

Beginning the ceremony, Sifu Mark lit three incense sticks, bowed, and holding them spoke in Chinese to the spirits and then in English saying that I was a good student and that I wanted to help people, so I was now going to teach qigong and help heal people. Next, he placed the incense in the brass burners and placed the card I had written on next to the center one. He then took his spirit fan from the altar and fanned me with it. and lit three more incense sticks and handed them to me. I bowed three times toward the altar and placed them in the burners. I declared that I would be a dedicated teacher and help people to the best of my ability. After this I had to *kow tow* to the altar, meaning I had to kneel down and bow, touching my forehead to the floor, three times. After rising from the floor, Sifu poured Chinese liquor into three little empty cups that were on the altar and gave them to me, one at a time, telling me to spill them out in a sweeping motion on the floor in front of the altar as I had seen him do during other ceremonies. Next, he handed me two silver heart-shaped pendants that hung on a silver chain and were always on the altar. They were inscribed on one side and blank on the other. He called them "spirit talkers." As I was taught, I swung them in a horizontal circle above the altar and then dropped them on the floor three times. Sifu's interpretation was positive—the spirits approved of my being a teacher and healer. He gave me the spirit fan I had made telling me to place it on my home altar.

When the ceremony was finished Master Mark took out a red book, he called *The Sky Book* and "looked up my bones" based on my birthdate, and time of birth. He wrote down something in Chinese on yellow joss paper then told me to also put it on my altar. Sifu then said he was going to write a letter for me as the traditional Chinese way to let people know I had his permission to teach. He told me what he wanted included in the letter and that I should go home and type it. When I finished the letter, I brought it to him. He asked me to read it aloud. He made a few changes and told me to retype it. In a couple of days, I brought the finished letter to him, read it aloud again. Happy with it this time, he signed it and put his stamp on it. He then wrote in calligraphy on rice paper that translates as, "Your inner self or heart's desire is your truest teacher." I had it framed and in hangs in our home chapel.

Soon after this, I was asked to teach two sections of qigong, as well as a basic counseling class at Northwestern Health Sciences University's Chinese Medicine College. The college wanted a letter of endorsement and the letter that Master Mark had written was perfect for this. I started teaching there and also began teaching a group of students on Thursday evenings in the downstairs of our split-level home where we had made a space for teaching and where I had set up an altar which Master Mark came to bless. He placed some ashes from the incense pot on his altar in my incense pot, explaining that it contained ashes from all of the previous masters of his school's lineage. I felt very honored and happy.

Even though I was now teaching qigong and incorporating it into my counseling work, something still seemed to be missing. Victoria Sweet describes a similar dilemma in her wonderful book, *Slow Medicine: The Way of Healing*. As she was reviewing the hospital care of her father, Dr. Sweet felt there was just something missing that was difficult for her to put her finger on. The words she finally found to describe it were, "medicine without a soul." Dr. Sweet's words resonated with what I was feeling. I was practicing psychotherapy without a soul.

It was Wendy, who guided me to begin this next phase of my hero's journey. I was still trying to resolve the unfinished business of my failed doctorate and had been accepted and begun a doctoral program in naturopathic medicine. After a couple of semesters however, while I enjoyed the courses, it just didn't seem to be the right program for me. In addition, I discovered that at that time, neither Wisconsin nor Minnesota licensed naturopathic doctors. So again, I applied the credits I had earned to another program

## Chapter Eight: The Way of the Shen Fu

and received a certificate in natural wellness for health care professionals. And again, I was troubled by dropping out of a doctoral program for a second time.

While conferring about what I should do next with Wendy, she took me by the hand and led me into my office. Once inside, she made a sweeping gesture with her hand, and said, "Look at all the books in your library. So many of them are about spirituality and religion. Maybe you should explore becoming a minister." At first, I rejected this idea out of hand. But after thinking about it for some time, I came to realize that she had an insight that somehow had eluded me. It was spirituality, the soul, in Dr. Sweet's words, that was at the core of what was missing from my practice and at the core of that which I had been chasing ever since the incident with my little daughter those many years earlier. The Pueblo chief, Santiago, knew that to be a healer one must be able to dance to the divine music that arises from deep within the soul. I wondered if to be truly healed, one also needed to dance to her or his own inner music. Even though I had learned shengong, I kept it completely separate from my counseling work. Synchronistically, at one of Master Hong's advanced workshops that I attended soon after Wendy's comment, he told us that as qigong healers, we are not doing something to the person who seeks our help, rather our spirit works with their spirit and qigong is like a spiritual dance with a partner. The problem I foresaw with this newly discovered interest, was that I doubted any traditional seminary would be a good match for me.

After a bit of investigating, I signed up for a day of discernment at United Theological Seminary in the Twin Cities. At the end of a busy day exploring the campus, listening to speakers, and prayer, I met individually with one of the seminary's advisors. He asked me about my faith tradition. I answered, and his long pause led me to believe he didn't know how to respond to my answer that I saw myself as a Christian Taoist. He suggested that I consider the Unitarian Universalist track at United or an interfaith seminary. After exploring the options, I had a telephone interview with one of the faculty at The New Seminary in New York City. I thought this was a program I could accept and enrolled in their interfaith ministry program with an emphasis on spiritual counseling.

One of the reasons I was attracted to the New Seminary was their belief that students should not only learn about world religions, but should also deepen their relationship with and understanding of their own faith tradition. "Never instead of, always in addition to" was the motto of Rabbi Joseph H. Gelberman, the founder of the New Seminary. He believed whatever one's faith tradition, they should go deeper into it. In addition, each student should open their heart, ears and minds to the wisdom found in other faiths and religious traditions. Rabbi Gelberman believed that the Holy One gave only some wisdom to each religion, so to know all of God's wisdom, we have to learn from each other. I had some very interesting discussions with one of the professors, Father Giles Spoonhour, a former Roman Catholic priest who left the priesthood to marry and was now a priest in the Orthodox-Catholic Church of America. He was able to relate to my Catholic upbringing as well as my concerns regarding some of the teachings of the Roman Catholic Church. The beautiful and memorable graduation and ordination was held at St. John the Divine Cathedral in New York City. During the dinner reception following the ceremony, Wendy and I sat at a table with Father Giles and his wife, Ann. While assuring me he wasn't trying to push me into anything, Fr. Giles suggested I check out the Orthodox-Catholic Church, as it incorporated some of the elements of Catholicism that I missed, while differing from the Roman Catholic Church in significant theological ways that he believed I would appreciate. That summer, I celebrated my first interfaith service at Woodbury United Methodist church. The pastor there, Doug Nicholas, had officiated at Wendy's and my wedding and had been a mentor, meeting regularly with me while I was in seminary. He even asked me to co-officiate a Lenten healing service at his church while I was a seminary student. Doug and I continued to be friends and to meet for coffee and theological discussions until his untimely and sad death in 2016.

Later that summer, Wendy and I discovered a small Orthodox-Catholic Church of America home church not too far from us. We attended a Sunday Holy Liturgy there and found the experience comforting and nostalgic. The priest, Father Jeff, was very welcoming and friendly. He even asked if I would like to preach a homily some Sunday. After attending the Holy Liturgy there for a while, Father Jeff and I met for lunch. He answered the questions I had about the Orthodox-Catholic Church's history and theology. During the course of our conversation, I asked what I would have to do to be considered for their program leading to ordination as an Orthodox-Catholic priest. Father Jeff told me he would speak with his bishop and get back to me.

A few weeks later, as Wendy and I were just arriving home from the grocery store and carrying our grocery bags into the house, my cell phone rang. I set down the bags I was carrying and answered. The caller identified himself as the metropolitan bishop of the Orthodox-Catholic Church of America. I thought it was Father Jeff, who could be a jokester, playing a trick on me and disguising his voice, so I answered, "Sure it is. Is that you Jeff?" The caller assured me that it was not Father Jeff and it was indeed the bishop. We spoke on the phone for about thirty minutes in an easy and comfortable manner. One of the things I discovered during that conversation that attracted me to the Orthodox tradition immediately, was that the Eastern Church never accepted the concept of original sin as taught by Augustine of Hippo. They believe that while we inherited and live in a world in which there is suffering and death, babies are not born with inherited sin. In fact, each child is born in the Divine image. The Eastern Christian Church seemed to agree with Celtic Saint Morgan of Wales, who taught that to look into the face of a newborn is to see the face of God. The bishop told me he had spoken with Father Jeff and Father Giles and that they both supported my desire to seek ordination. He recommended that I read the book, *Common Ground: An Introduction to Eastern Christianity for the American Christian* by Jordan Balis and then talk with Father Jeff if I decided I would like to proceed. While reading this book, I discovered that the Eastern approach to Christianity was much more acceptable to me at the time than the Western teachings with which I grew up.

There was one glaring obstacle that I thought would certainly prevent my being allowed to enter seminary and become a priest. Even though Eastern Orthodox priests can be married, I was divorced and remarried. Father Jeff told me that this did not automatically disqualify me. The Orthodox-Catholic Church believed that in the words of Jesus, "I will give you the keys to the kingdom of heaven. What you lock on earth will be locked in heaven. What you unlock on earth will be unlocked in heaven" (Matthew 16:19) gave the Church the authority to "unlock" one's marriage vows. I decided to seek admission to the presbyter training program and after their vetting process was completed, that included a private interview with Wendy, I was admitted to the program. Father Jeff was assigned as my mentor and the director of the Pastoral Theology Institute, put together a course of study for me. As I neared the end of the program, I spoke with Father Jeff and a friend who was a Benedictine nun about concerns I had regarding some of the language of the Nicene Creed which I would have to recite, professing my agreement, during my ordination. Sister Lois recommended the book *In Search of Belief* by Joan Chittister. I took her advice and found Sister Joan's interpretations of the statements in the Creed made sense to me and I could live with these statements as she broadly interpreted them. In addition, whenever I expressed doubt in one of the sections of the Creed, Father Jeff would say, "What do you think about that statement?" After explaining my view, he would always pause, think for a minute, and then say that my point of view was an acceptable way to think about it.

## Chapter Eight: The Way of the Shen Fu

As usual that summer, Wendy and I took a vacation at Solbakken Resort staying in cozy cabin 4. One night as we sat by a bonfire on the rock ledge sipping Baileys and coffee, Wendy asked me, "Why do you want to be a priest?" I replied that I guess, somewhere deep inside, I have always wanted to be a priest, ever since I was a young boy pretending to say Mass at home, and certainly since I was an altar boy. I continued to explain that while I value the interfaith philosophy that honors the many paths to the Holy and acknowledges that there is truth in each one, the heart of my spiritual life has always been the Way of Jesus, and my seeing him in my near-death experience reinforced that relationship. I continued by telling Wendy my story as I shared it with you in Chapter two.

The next night, sitting by the fire at Solbakken again, Wendy asked "Who will you serve as a priest?" As I thought about it, the answer that kept coming into my mind, to this obvious variation on the grail question, "Who does the Grail serve" was, "I serve the brokenhearted." Then she asked, "Who are the brokenhearted?" The words of Isaiah, the Hebrew prophet, that Jesus quoted as he began his own work, came to mind. "The Holy One has sent me to heal the brokenhearted; to proclaim freedom to the captives, to let out into light those bound in the dark; to proclaim the year of the favor of God, and to comfort all who mourn." From a depth psychology perspective, captivity could be a metaphor referring to that which holds us prisoner emotionally or psychologically. To let out into the light, the shadows hidden in the unconscious and guide them into enlightenment. Images of people I had known surfaced: Those who had lost a loved one to death, divorce, or abandonment; Those who feel unloved; Those who had been rejected by their church; Those who felt lost; Those who were afraid; Those who were weighted down by chronic or life-threatening illness; Those who felt they had committed some unforgivable past action. As a priest I could also offer the sacraments of confession and anoint people as I did in my dream years earlier.

That summer, on July 29, 2007, I was ordained as an Orthodox-Catholic priest in a lovely and meaningful ceremony surrounded by family and friends. A highlight for me was having Wendy and Father Jeff robe me with the stole and chasuble of priesthood and then co-celebrating the Divine Liturgy with Metropolitan Bishop Carsten. During his homily, the bishop talked about my Hungarian surname, Lacska, being a derivation of the name Lazarus, the friend of Jesus who in John's gospel had died and who Jesus called forth from his tomb and said to those gathered in mourning, "Unbind him, let him go free." Priesthood, the bishop said, was a calling forth into a new life, of being born again. His message was especially poignant because of the near-death experience I had as a child. I too, like Lazarus, was brought back from death, and while it took me over forty years to arrive at this place in my life, I felt free to dance to the music of the Spirit within. Now the dream I had ten years earlier, during my shengong training, was being repeated in my awake life. I was a priest, and as I looked out from the altar toward those gathered to support me, Wendy was sitting in the same place as she was in my dream. And another verse from the song, Amazing Grace that I sang in that dream, presented itself to me: *Through many dangers, toils and snares, I have already come; 'tis grace hath brought me safe thus far, and grace will lead me home.*

## Chapter Nine

# *Spirits, Ghosts, and Dreams*

When you are on the right path,
invisible hands will come to your aid.
Joseph Campbell

In the myths and folk tales around the world, the hero often encounters ghosts or spirits who provide help or guidance. These encounters can occur when the hero is awake or in a dream. In Homer's Odyssey, the hero Odysseus enters the underworld to seek help from the ghost of the blind prophet Tiresias to find his way back to Ithaca. While in the underworld, Odysseus encounters other ghosts, including the ghost of his mother. In the modern mythic story, *Star Wars*, Luke Skywalker is visited by the ghost of his mentor, Obi-Wan Kenobi, who tries to dissuade him from attempting to rescue his friends. Probably the most famous literary encounter with ghosts and spirits occurs is Charles Dickens' beloved story, *A Christmas Carol*, in which Ebenezer Scrooge is visited by the ghost of his deceased business partner, and then by three Christmas spirits. In the Christian gospel story from Luke, a young woman named Miryam (Mary) is visited by an angel who informs her that she will bear a child by the *Ruach HaKodesh* (Holy Spirit) (1:35). In the gospel of Matthew, Mary's betrothed, Yosef (Joseph), is visited in a dream by an angel who tells him "Yosef, son of David, do not be afraid to take Miryam home with you as your wife; for what has been conceived in her is from the Ruach HaKodesh (1:20).

This idea of ethereal helpers was a basic premise of my shengong training with Master Mark and was certainly not a foreign concept to me having been raised in the Roman Catholic tradition. Seeking help from an abundant assemblage of otherworldly beings was a common practice. There was Jesus, the Blessed Mother, the angels, including a personal guardian angel, and the saints. Of course, when things got really tough, we could go straight to the top, God the Father, who even as a child, looked suspiciously like Zeus and Odin. I had two precursory childhood acquaintances with otherworldly spirits that made them very real for me. The first was my near-death experience that I shared in chapter two. The second was related to the severe migraine headaches I occasionally had as a child. When I would get one of these very bad headaches, Mom would do all she could to help. She gave me aspirin and rubbed some kind of herbal poultice on my forehead and temples and then tied a bandana tightly around my head to hold it in place. But in my young mind, the real cure for these headaches came from the Blessed Mother. Once I was tucked into bed by my parents, I would say three Hail Mary's and then with all the devoutness I could muster, I would finish with the Memorare:

Remember, O most gracious Virgin Mary, that never was it known that anyone who fled to thy protection, implored thy help, or sought thine intercession was left unaided.

Inspired by this confidence, I fly unto thee, O Virgin of Virgins, my mother; to thee I come, before thee I stand, sinful and sorrowful. O Mother of the Word Incarnate, despise not my petitions, but in thy mercy, hear and answer me. Amen.

When I followed this routine, I would always quickly fall asleep, and when I woke up, my headache would be gone. There was no doubt in my child's mind, that it was the Blessed Mother that took away my headache. I must admit that as an adult being wheeled into the operating room for open heart surgery, I was again praying the Memorare.

## Chapter Nine: Spirits, Ghosts, and Dreams

During my freshman and sophomore years of college, I became interested in parapsychology. I was fascinated by what researchers at Duke University, Stanford, and UCLA, were theorizing about ghosts, poltergeists, extra-sensory perception, and other psychic phenomena. Investigations were being carried out to try to determine whether hauntings could be verified and explained scientifically. While I was an undergraduate student in Luxembourg, there was a rumor floating around that one of the rooms in an adjacent hallway of the Ansembourg Castle, in which the school was located, was haunted. The students staying in that room had been moved out. I typed a proposal on my old Smith-Corona manual typewriter, asking permission to sleep in the room in question with another student to determine if some rational explanation could be found for the phenomenon, or whether it was a hoax being perpetrated by one or more of the students. Permission was granted by the dean of students, so one of my roommates and I made preparations in the room, mimicking those I had read about in parapsychology books. We covered the window so nothing could be projected or shined in from outside. We sprinkled white flour on the window sills and on the floor inside and outside the room, and we placed cellophane tape between the door and the door jamb so that anyone opening the door besides us would break the seal. I was also armed with my trusty Kodak Hawkeye Instamatic camera and a flashlight. My roommate and I planned to take turns staying awake throughout the night. We didn't tell any other students what we were doing. We were convinced we would discover whatever or whoever was "haunting" the room and hallway.

As evening approached, we sat in the room studying, but keeping alert for anything "unusual." Just past midnight, the temperature in the room suddenly dropped quickly. It got cold enough that we could see our breath as we exhaled. We immediately checked the window for drafts, but none was coming through it. Then, in the corner of the room, opposite the door across the room from where we were sitting, a white vaporous substance began to manifest, slowly taking on a human size and shape. We could see a vague torso, and below that, a tenuous form of a dress. The shape of shoulders and a head emerged, but there were no clearly definable features. Then the figurer figure slowly moved, floating across the room and disappearing through the closed door. Quickly checking our ghost traps, we could see the door had not been tampered with and there were no footprints in the white flour we had placed on the floor on both sides of the door. We went into the hallway and scanning in both directions could see that no one else was there. The "ghost" had moved down the hall and began to descend the spiral stairs of the turret at the end of the hall. We then realized, that in our excitement and apprehensiveness, we had not taken any photos. A few days later, I saw Count Gaston, who owned the castle, walking on the grounds. I asked him if he knew of any ghost stories associated with the castle. He told me of a famous story about a young maiden who was to be married found out that her fiancé was killed in battle shortly before his scheduled return for their wedding. In her shock and grief, she left her room in the castle at midnight, walked up the path behind the castle to the family chapel, and there, committed suicide. I asked if he knew where her room was located. He didn't know because there had been so much remodeling to the chateau over the years. But then, he pointed to the section of the building where we had seen the apparition, saying that it was somewhere in that section of the chateau. He concluded by saying that many people have reported seeing her ghost over the years.

I am in good company, having experienced a haunting. In 1920, Carl Jung was invited to England to share his theories. He lodged in a cottage that was available at a surprisingly inexpensive rate. Jung noticed that the maids always made a point to leave the house before sunset. Inquiring why they did this, they told him that the cottage was haunted. Jung later reported that while in bed one night, he heard noises and had the feeling there was something near him. When he opened his eyes, beside him, on the bed, he saw an old woman, her wide-open eyes staring at him. Terrified, he bolted out of the bed and lit a candle. Checking the room thoroughly, he saw no one. He spent the rest of the night in an armchair. The following morning, he moved into a different room, where he reported that he slept comfortably without further ghostly incidents for the remainder of his stay. This story was published in a book by Fanny Moser, for which Jung wrote the preface. Another ghostly incident occurred in 1924, while Jung was staying at his retreat tower in Bollingen on Lake Zurich. He heard footsteps as if from a large group, and voices singing around the tower during the night. He looked out the window but saw nothing. This happened several more times throughout the night, but upon looking, he never saw anyone. Sometime later, Jung came across a seventeenth century document written by someone else who had the same experience while he was spending the night in the same location. The author noted that the area was known for apparitions and that the locals believed that it was Wotan's army of departed warriors (qtd. in Jung on Synchronicity and the Paranormal). Toward the end of his life, Jung was quoted as saying, "I myself cannot brag about any original research in this field, but declare without hesitation that I was able to witness enough of these phenomena to be wholly convinced that they are real. However, I cannot explain them, and hence cannot decide on any of the usual interpretations" (Jaffé 1968).

Wendy and I had our own ghostly encounter. The story begins on a visit to Mayo clinic to see my ophthalmologist. After my appointment, we decided to eat at Victoria's, a very fine Italian restaurant in Rochester—just a block away from the clinic. It was around three o'clock in the afternoon and only two other tables were occupied at that time. In a booth kitty-corner from ours was a tall gentleman and his wife who looked to be in their sixties. All of a sudden, we heard the man say that he had a headache and he put his hand to his forehead. Then suddenly, he fell over against the wall next to their booth. The woman called for help. For a moment, I was stunned, but Wendy quickly said, "You know first aid and CPR, go over and help." I rushed over, telling the server to call 911, and then lowered the man to the floor. Wendy came over and stood next to his wife to offer support. Checking, I found a pulse, but he was not breathing, so I nervously started rescue breathing. After several breaths, I stopped, turned my head, and looked down at his chest to see if he had begun breathing on his own. As I looked for any rising and falling of his chest, indicating that he was breathing on his own, I saw a kind of shimmering vapor, like you see coming off hot pavement after it rains, and I wondered if that was his spirit or soul leaving his body. I continued rescue breathing until the emergency responders arrived and took over.

As soon as the ambulance left, Wendy said that we had to go to the emergency room at St. Mary's Hospital to be with the man's wife. Wendy had learned that the couple were from Iowa and had driven to Mayo for the man to receive medical treatment. His wife was now all alone. When we arrived at the emergency room, and after some smooth talking, a nurse brought us back to a small private waiting room where the woman from the restaurant was sitting with a chaplain. She was crying. As soon as she saw Wendy, she jumped up and hugged her, thanking us for coming to be with her. Holding back tears, she told us that her husband, whose name was Bill, had died and she was waiting for family members to drive up from Iowa. We stayed with her until a family member arrived a few hours later. Before we left for home, Wendy and I decided to stop at the beautiful St. Mary's chapel to pray for the family. When we finally arrived at home, there was a book in our mailbox. A doctor I had recently met, put the book in our mailbox, knowing about my interest in qigong and healing. The book was *Shaman, Healer, Sage: How to Heal Yourself and Others with the Energy Medicine of the Americas*, by Alberto Villoldo, a psychologist and medical anthropologist. When we got inside the house and settled in, I sat down, with a cup of tea, opened the book, and started reading from chapter one. It was the author's recollection of being with a South American shaman at the death of a woman. He wrote: "Something glimmered along the surface of her body, something milky and translucent an inch or so above the body's contour . . . and there it was, out of focus but clearly there, an ever so subtle glow . . . as if a luminous mold of her body was emerging from the flesh." O my God! I called to Wendy, and read this passage aloud to her. It was a description of what I had just seen looking down at Bill's body while performing rescue breathing.

A few days after this event, Wendy was hanging clothes downstairs in our laundry room when I heard her frightened yell, calling for me. I rushed down, wondering what was wrong. When I came into the laundry room she ran into my arms. I asked what had happened. She told me that while she was hanging clothes, she thought I had come downstairs and put my arms around her giving her a hug from behind, but when she turned around it was not me. It was an apparition of a big tall man. I immediately said, "Oh, that was probably Bill saying thank you for helping his wife. She thought that I was probably right, but didn't want him hanging around the house. She asked me to do something so that Bill's ghostly energy would leave the house and move on to where he belonged.

Chinese medicine, religious traditions, and physics, all agree that our world is surrounded by and filled with energy. Sometimes, a painful incident, such as illness or death, an act of violence, or an unhappy or abusive marriage ending in divorce, leaves residual energy that can linger in a home or business. Along my journey as a priest, I have been asked on a few occasions to perform a house blessing, or clearing, for someone who believed that their house or business was either haunted, or had very negative energy in it. In some cases, the people had seen the ghost or spirit of someone who was deceased, like Wendy had in our laundry room. In one case a violent crime had been committed in a small business in our home town. When a new business opened in that space, the employees felt anxiety and fear inside the building. At one home, a little girl of about five or six asked me, "Are you going to get the old man to leave?" When I asked her about the "old man" she told me that she sometimes sees an old man with a beard and he was crabby. She didn't go into any further detail. I asked the adults about this, and while they were reluctant to speak of it, they had also seen an apparition of an old bearded man, who none of them recognized. The ceremony I use to clear negative energy and bless a space combines a shengong ritual I learned from Master Mark with an Eastern Orthodox house blessing ceremony. In every single situation in which I have used this ritual, the home or business owners have reported that the negative feeling or ghostly presence was gone after the ritual was performed. I have no idea how this really works, but the elements of this ritual, that have been used for over a thousand years, somehow do work. In one case, the home owners later reported to me that friends, who knew nothing of the ritual being performed, came to their house for dinner a few days after the house blessing. They asked if the owners had painted the interior of their home because the place felt so much "lighter." They had not painted or done anything besides cleansing the negative or unwanted energy. After doing the ritual at our home, we never saw or felt Bill's presence again.

Another domain that I have found to be very helpful on my hero's journey and in my integrative and transpersonal approach to counseling is working with dreams. Interestingly, the word "dream" is related to the Old Norse word *draugr* meaning ghost or apparition. So, at least for my Scandinavian maternal ancestors, ghosts and dreams correspond. The ancient Greeks from the fifth through first centuries BCE built temples in honor of Asclepius, the Greek god of healing. A major component of healing was through what the Greeks termed dream incubation. Priest-physicians at these temples, skilled in the practice of healing, ritual, and dream interpretation were present to aid pilgrims. Those seeking healing participated in

## Chapter Nine: Spirits, Ghosts, and Dreams

purification rites and other rituals meant to facilitate a dream of the gods that would bring about either immediate healing, or elucidate the cause of their illness and give insight into what was necessary for healing to take place. Dream incubation, in a modified Christian form, is still practiced in a few remote Greek Orthodox monasteries.

For Carl Jung, dreams were hidden doorways into the most intimate depths of our soul. Dreams can serve to reveal hidden areas of the unconscious, helping us deepen our awareness of the wisdom within us. The psalmist wrote, "I bless Adonai, my counselor; at night my inmost being instructs me" (16:7). As she was coming near to her death, Kari, a dear friend and colleague, shared a dream with me. In her dream, she was chasing a fairy who she knew had a question she needed to hear. When she finally caught the fairy, the question the fairy asked was, "Do you want to unhook the latches?" In her dream, Kari answered, yes. The fairy then told her that they are hidden, and she had to find them to unlatch them. Then the sprite flew away. Kari searched and found a couple of latches and unlatched them and the dream ended. We talked about what this dream might mean and through an active imagination exercise with the dream fairy, my friend realized that the dream was telling her she still needed to "unlatch" and release certain attachments that her body and ego feared letting go of, so she could die peacefully. I asked her if she would like help with this. She responded positively, and so we worked on discovering these attachments together and ritually letting them go. Our work reminded me of the words of Joyce Rockwood Hudson in her book, *Natural Spirituality: Recovering the Wisdom Tradition in Christianity*. She wrote, "Dreams show us our truth as it really is, not as our minds think it should be nor as our hearts would like it to be, but as it truly is. To walk hand in hand with our dreams is to walk with the Spirit of truth, with an understanding that comes to us directly from the realm of the living God" (81). My friend's dream and her willingness to work on releasing her attachments brought a new and powerful awareness that one of my roles as a counselor and priest was to be a midwife of the soul, helping the dying individual's soul to be born into the next world.

Besides being helped and guided by ghosts, maybe we can also help them. Wendy once had a dream in which a friend's ghost, who had died a violent death when they were both young teachers, came to our house and was very sad. Wendy was troubled by the dream. We prayed at our altar that if Jane needed healing, she was welcome to stay and we would do a ceremony for her. We did conduct a ceremony for Jane and Wendy also made a small garden spot to honor her. A few days later, Wendy couldn't find a case of Olio Santo Olive Oil she bought. We looked everywhere, over and over again. She went to our home altar and asked Jane for help. Immediately after asking, Wendy got up without saying a word, walked into the guest bedroom, opened the closet, moved a Navaho rug aside, and there was the oil. We had looked in the closet at least twice, but had never moved the rug aside far enough. Wendy was sure that somehow Jane had helped her find the oil. Maybe our relationships with spirits and ghosts are reciprocal.

In the late summer and early autumn of 2012, Wendy and I enjoyed a six-week holiday in England and Scotland. We spent four days of our trip on the island of Iona, one of the Inner Hebrides off the west coast of Scotland. Iona has been a popular pilgrim site for centuries. Iona is also considered by many to be a "thin place" where, as the Celts say, the veil is thin between the world of matter and the world of spirit. While we were there, I had two powerful dreams. In the first dream, I am getting ready to celebrate the Holy Liturgy at Iona Abbey and realize I don't know where to find an alb and stole nor what the readings are for the day. Now, this part of the dream is familiar to me. I have had dreams of being unprepared many times with variations of place and people. But in this dream, instead of ending with feelings of confusion and inadequacy, I am approached by an old man with long white hair and beard. He is wearing a long white robe and I know he is a priest. He puts a hand on my shoulder and says that all of the things, such as how I am dressed or what the readings are don't really matter, and I should just open up and speak from my heart and all will be well. He then pats me on the shoulder and walks away. This was a healing dream. Since then, I have not had any dreams about being unprepared, or not knowing what to do. In my second dream on Iona, I am in the Abbey again, and Master Hong Liu is there with me. He tells me that this (Iona) is a very powerful place of qi and that Saint Martin's Cross is especially powerful for me because of my ancestry. He then says I should practice standing meditation at the base of the stone cross. The dream ends. For me, Saint Martin of Tours, the namesake of the cross in the courtyard of the abbey, has special significance. He was a fourth-century Roman cavalry soldier from the Celtic region that is now Hungary, the land of my paternal ancestors. St. Martin was also the saint's name I took at confirmation as a boy. I also had a powerful dream of St Martin at the retreat just prior to my ordination at St John the Divine Cathedral. So, at twilight the next day, I stood in qigong meditation at the foot of St. Martin's cross. It was a powerful and emotionally moving experience for me.

Wendy also had an extraordinary vision on Iona. One evening, as we sat in the abbey chapel for evensong, Wendy closed her eyes, enjoying the Celtic music. All of a sudden, she had a vision that the abbey was like a large English train station. She could see people scurrying about, going on trains to different destinations, but no one else could see them. All of a sudden, her deceased friend Jane was standing next to her. Then Wendy saw her father, who died when she was a college student, approaching her from one of the platforms. Once he joined them, Wendy introduced her father to Jane and they began to have a friendly conversation. Jane and her dad walked off together. Wendy said she had a comforting feeling that somehow, they were now free.

Do the ghosts of deceased people really appear in dreams to help us on our journeys? I told the story of my dad appearing in a dream after his death to reassure me that he would always be with me. Another friend of mine who died from cancer also appeared in a dream, telling me what it was like to be in the spirit world and how it was difficult to communicate with people who were still in their bodies. Recent scientific studies tell us that more than half of the population of the United States report seeing a deceased relative or friend shortly after the person's death in a dream or a vision. A series of new studies reported that almost all people have experiences of seeing deceased individuals just before their own deaths. As a psychologist, I understand that these dreams or visions of deceased people could be images created by our own minds, drawing upon meaningful people and archetypal images to help us sort things out and be comforted. But like Jung, I can't decide what is really happening. I know that I cannot rule out that the spirits of deceased individuals who love us, may appear in dreams to help and guide us. Another incident involved Kari, the medical doctor, colleague, and friend who I mentioned before, and with whom I co-facilitated a cancer support group. She had developed end-stage cancer and asked me to help her through her cancer journey by counseling her and with qigong to help relieve the side effects of her medication and with her pain as the disease progressed.

As her journey neared the end, she asked me to officiate at her memorial when the time came. She wanted me to preside over a Holy Liturgy and to get someone to incorporate an indigenous pipe ceremony into it. This was important to her because in addition to her MD degree, she had studied indigenous healing with a Native American healer. After she passed, I asked a friend who was a traditional pipe carrier to do this and he agreed. Unfortunately, the day before the memorial, he called to tell me that he was ill and would not be able do it. He offered to tell me how to use the pipe respectfully to pray in the four directions and bless the family. I told him that, not being an indigenous person, I did not feel comfortable doing this. That night I had the following dream: I'm walking in a grassy field with Kari. It is a warm and sunny day and her dog, who died shortly after her, is running around near us, occasionally darting off to chase a squirrel. We come to a round wooden picnic table with benches on two sides. Wendy is sitting on one of the benches. As we sit down, I all of a sudden realize that Kari and her dog are both dead. I am excited and happy. I turn to look at Wendy and say, "Can you believe this? Kari is here!" But Wendy has disappeared, as did the surroundings, just as it did in the dream about my father. Everything is gone except the table, Kari and me, and the benches we are sitting on. I ask her how she is and about life after death. She explains that it's not very different from when you are in your body. I tell her about the memorial we are planning for her and that I couldn't arrange for a pipe ceremony. She is insistent that I should use the sacred pipe myself and not to worry about whether any indigenous people present will think it is inappropriate. She trusts it will be just right. I touch her arm and it feels somehow both substantial and yet intangible, and tell her I will do as she requests and bless her family with the sacred pipe. The dream ended. I shared this dream with my pipe carrier friend who said that I must honor Kari's wishes and he proceeded to teach me how to use the pipe respectfully.

At the memorial Holy Liturgy, after the opening prayers and a litany of remembrances, I unwrapped the pipe and placed it on a red cloth on the altar as directed. I smudged the bowl, stem, tobacco, and other items, including myself, with sage. After praying with the pipe in the four directions, and up to the heavens and down to Mother Earth, I walked around clockwise, touching the pipe to each family member's shoulders and heart. When this was finished, I smoked the remaining tobacco in the bowl. Then, holding the pipe above my head, thanked the Creator, Grandmother Earth, each of the Powers of the Four Winds, and any other spirits or ancestors who were present. I acknowledged all beings in the cosmos by saying the Lakota phrase *Mitakuye Oyasin* (all my relations), acknowledging that we are indeed all related. I separated the bowl and the stem, removed the ashes and wrapped the pipe, setting it on the side of the altar, signifying that the pipe ceremony was now completed. Then I continued with the celebration of the Holy Eucharist. The next morning, I had a dream in which Kari was talking on her cell phone. In a lucid dream moment, I thought to myself, "Who does she think she's talking with? She's dead." Then I woke up and, in that half-asleep, half-awake state, rolled over and saw Kari squatting down leaning against the wall and smiling. I did not react in shock or fear. I just said, "Oh, there you are." Her image, or ghost, faded from view, and I went back to sleep.

In another dream, my Metropolitan Bishop, who had recently died, was with me. He tells me that I have a unique calling and that I must be bold enough to follow this calling which is out of the typical ministry box, because there is a great need for what I have to offer. Then, he begins helping me sort through boxes in a large room that is filled with a variety of objects with religious or spiritual significance. Some of these objects are things I actually own. Skip tells me that I must decide which ones I need to keep to take on my journey and which I must leave behind.

My Dad also showed up again in a dream when I couldn't make up my mind about whether I should go to Los Angeles to see Master Hong Liu for the first time. In the dream, I am on a green grassy hill, reminiscent of the one in the near-death experience of my childhood. The field overlooks a beautiful resort in the distance. I see Dad and someone else walking up the hill and as he gets closer, I see that he is with Bing Crosby. Dad introduces me to Bing who is funny and friendly, and we all sing one of his songs together. The lyrics are: "*You gotta accentuate the positive. Eliminate the negative. Latch on to the affirmative. Don't mess with Mr. In-Between.*" When we finished the song, Dad says, to me, "Do you get it?" He then says they have to go back, but I can't come along. I wake up.

## Chapter Nine: Spirits, Ghosts, and Dreams

For few years, early in our marriage, Wendy was the art teacher at the American Indian Magnet School in St. Paul. While she was working there, we were invited by one of the Lakota staff to participate in a ceremony for two people who were preparing to go on a vision quest. A Lakota Holy man, Elmer Running, was coming to lead the *Yuwipi* (calling in) ceremony. We bought some cookies to share at the potluck after the ceremony and some tobacco to offer to Elmer, as he asked to be called. That night would prove to be a unique and powerful spiritual experience for us. Elmer Running was one of the first men to participate in the revived Sun Dance in modern times. This holy man urged everyone to develop a relationship with spirit guides to help them along life's path. Elmer set up his altar on the floor in the center of the room around a small Navaho rug on which he sat or kneeled in seiza throughout the ceremony. Everyone else was seated around the room, backs against the walls. All of the windows and seams along the door were sealed with black trash bags and tape. We had to remove our shoes and all jewelry and metal objects and put them in a pocket or under the sleeping bag or blanket we brought to sit on. When all was ready, the vision questers presented their pipes to Elmer formally requesting his assistance. Then the room and all sacred objects were smudged, we rubbed sage on ourselves and put a twig of sage behind our ear. Then Elmer directed that the lights be turned off. It was pitch black. We literally could not see our hand if we put it in front of our face. Singing began accompanied by a hand drum. When the song ended, Elmer spoke, explaining the ceremony. Then he prayed in Lakota for a long time and when he finished, he called for the "spirit calling song" to be sung. As the song was being sung, suddenly throughout the room, little blue-white spheres of light began to appear. Some of them were just slightly bigger than fireflies, and others were about the size of a softball. Their entrance was accompanied by the sound of rushing wind and rattling as if a rattle was moving in stereo from one side of the room to the other. There were no speakers nor any sound system in the room. I could feel Wendy's fingers digging into my thigh. She leaned close and whispered, "Do you see them?" I whispered back, "I do." There was also the sound like an eagle bone whistle moving across and around the room accompanied by wind blowing across our faces as if a large bird just flew by in front of us. There was more singing and prayers; each person praying in turn around the room, beginning with Elmer's wife and ending with Elmer. After he prayed, the spirits left, seemingly through the walls. After a closing song and prayer, the lights were turned on and we shared the potluck dinner. The ceremony had lasted four hours. No one, except us, thought the appearance of blue lights was unusual. When we asked about it, we were told that this always happens at ceremonies.

The next evening, Wendy and I were invited back for another ceremony led by Elmer. This time we were told to make 50 red prayer ties, 12 white ones, and 12 yellow ones to bring to the ceremony. When we arrived, we were still making them. A nice couple took pity on us and showed us an easier way to make the tobacco ties and they also looked much neater. Wendy sat with the couple and also made 6 green and 6 blue ties for Spotted Eagle, one of Elmer's spirit helpers. This memory would come back strongly a couple of years later when I encountered Master Mark's spirit helper, Golden Eagle, at his altar. There were many strands of prayer ties, with hundreds of each color, laid in long lines next to Elmer. On each of the four corners of Elmer's Navaho rug, stood a colored prayer flag, one for each of the four directions. This night was a healing ceremony and the spirits again were very present. There were more blue-white lights/spirits than were present on previous night. At one point, I could see one of the lights right above Wendy's and my heads. While the sphere glowed with light, it did not illuminate anything around it nor did it cast any shadow. When the lights were turned on at the end of the ceremony, all of the strands of prayer ties had somehow become braided together in an obvious pattern of colors, and they were sitting on the floor in a circle in

## Chapter Nine: Spirits, Ghosts, and Dreams

front of the person who was seeking healing. Reflecting on this over the years, I wonder if this was what happened at Pentecost as described in the Acts of the Apostles. "Suddenly a sound like the howling of the wind filled the entire house where they were sitting. They saw what seemed to be individual flames of fire alighting on each one of them" (2:2-3). Were the flames of fire the same as the blue lights we had seen? Ever since then, I have pondered why this indigenous ritual has such power. Why do spirits manifest in Native American ceremonies and at Master Mark's altar, but do not appear during Christian, or other modern religious rituals, at least that I have ever heard tell. Perhaps as Christianity in the West became more of an organized religion and empire than a way of living, and theology and intellectualism became more important than mysticism, the magic was no longer experienced.

At the beginning of the new millennium, I discovered that I needed a total hip replacement. The orthopedic surgeon thought my hip joint wore out at a fairly young age due to a slight misalignment that had probably been present from birth. I decided to wait as long as I could before having surgery. Wendy and I had planned a vacation on the North Shore of Lake Superior and as usual, wanted to hike on the Superior Hiking Trail. The pain in my hip was going to make that a challenge. A teacher friend told me about a woman from South America who was a teaching assistant at her school and was a healer. I decided to visit her to see if she could relieve the pain in my hip, allowing me to hike with less pain. She knew nothing about me, not even my name, only that the teacher at her school told me about her. When I arrived, she led me into a small bedroom in her suburban house that she used as her treatment room. A massage table was in the center of the room and the walls were decorated with indigenous art. There was a statue of the Blessed Virgin on a small table with a vase of flowers in front of it. She told me that she was raised Catholic, but has had this ability to help people from the time she was a child. She asked me to remove my sandals and sit on the edge of the massage table. I had a difficult time bending down to do this. She offered to remove my sandals for me, but my masculine ego kicked in and I told her I could do it. When She saw how much pain it caused to bend down, she gently helped remove them for me. There was a great deal of empathy and compassion in her manner and in her energy work. As she was working, she said that there were spirits present and one was my guardian angel. Then she announced that I had been touched by Christ when I was a child. After a brief pause, she continued, saying that I had died and saw Jesus, but then came back. She also said that I was called to be a healer and that I needed to get out of my head and trust my intuition. All of a sudden, she started speaking in Spanish. After a while, she stopped speaking and said, "Your mother speaks Spanish. She is here too." She would have no way of knowing that my mother grew up in Panama and spoke fluent Spanish. I wept. Finally, she told me that I needed to open up my heart energy. Technique is good, she said, but I must open my spiritual heart to be a better healer. The next day, Wendy and I went on our vacation and I was able to hike without pain.

At one of Master Hong's advanced classes, we learned qigong exercises for joining our spirits with the universal spirit or God. At one of our practice sessions, he saw me making the hand gestures I saw him make while he was sending qi. He asked me why I was doing that. I told him I was following his example. He told me that I should use the power symbols and gestures from my own spiritual tradition. Then he made the sign of the cross in the air, saying, "Like this." That weekend, we learned that healing is not doing something to someone who needs help. Healing involves having our spirit communicate with the suffering person's spirit for diagnosis and then work with their spirit in the healing work. One of Master Hong's apprentices who was at this workshop is a psychiatrist. We had a good talk about combining qigong with psychotherapy. I asked him if he believed in literal rather than archetypal or metaphorical spirits. He responded that he didn't used to, but after working with Master Hong for several years, he now does. So again, I can relate to Carl Jung, being able to state without hesitation, that I have witnessed enough to be wholly convinced that what I have seen is real. However, like Jung, I cannot explain it, and therefore, cannot with full confidence, decide on any definitive interpretations or explanations for these phenomena. Ultimately, I have determined that whether I know definitively what has happened in a certain experience of mine, or with a person who has come to me for help, makes little difference. What matters is whether they feel better and whether I or they have gained insight that helps them in their life and on their own hero's journey from our work together. It was at this point that I could no longer refer to the individuals with whom I worked as clients. The term client seemed to place the emphasis on the financial relationship. A client is a customer. I began to use the term counselee. A counselee is simply a person seeking counseling.

With our constant reliance and exposure to the electronic world of our cell phones, the internet and social media, we've lost the valuable skill that our ancestors had of gathering information firsthand from our dreams and being attuned to guidance from the transcendent world. In his book *The Alchemist*, Paulo Coelho writes how the king tells the young pilgrim, Santiago that there is a language in the world that everyone understands, but has forgotten. It seems as though the Divine's mother tongue is primordial, most often speaking through images in dreams and through synchronicity, which we will explore in the next chapter. Psychiatrist Gerald May teaches that dreams are often the pathway into the deep and often shrouded areas within our psyche. Dreams can also reveal the work of the Divine within. Wendy and I celebrated our thirty-first anniversary this summer, and as is our custom, we looked through our "wedding box" containing our wedding memorabilia, Wendy took out the journal she was writing in around the time of our wedding and honeymoon. Browsing through it, she said, "Look, you wrote on the last pages of my journal. A notation before my entry indicated I had filled my own journal and Wendy allowed me to write down a big dream I had about one year after our wedding day. Estelle Frankel tells us dreams can aid us in becoming more cognizant of "who we are and who we might become," (133). While I had no idea at the time, this dream was a harbinger of what I might become on my hero's journey.

In my dream I have been called to help some children who were reporting paranormal experiences. Mysterious things were happening at the place where they would play. I was to determine what was happening and if there were environmental, social, or mental health issues involved. I met the kids and we went to the place where they experienced this uncanny phenomenon. I immediately felt a powerful sense of fear and the hairs on the back of my neck stood up. The dream scene changed. I was attempting to enter a large old university library building where I would search for answers. But each time I tried to enter, the double doors would close on me from both sides, trapping me so I could not enter. If I pulled back, the doors would loosen, but each time I tried to enter, the doors would trap me. An old custodian, helped me to force the doors open enough so I could squeeze through. I was then faced with a long dimly lit corridor. Large vines lined the walls. As I tried to go down the corridor, the vines would grab at my arms and legs. I asked about another way to enter, but the old man said that this was the only way in. I thought that maybe, if I run, I can make it through. I start running down the corridor, but the vines grabbed me, wrapping around my legs, arms, and neck, and I quickly realize that my legs and arms were being cut off by the tightening vines, dismembering me, and that I would die. The scene changes again. I am in the ruins of an ancient temple. There is a woman there who has magical abilities. She is touching the rubble and asking me to touch it also. She says there is a powerful force there. The scene changes again. The woman and I are back at the entrance to the library building. She shows me that how we position our hands in space influences the energy around us. Again, the doors try to keep us out, but how we hold our hands effects the doors and we can enter. I think this energy must be some type of natural phenomenon that I just don't understand. The scene changes once more. Now I am a doctor helping a woman who just delivered a baby. I can't see her face. I feel panicked because I am not a real doctor. Then I feel the presence of this energy or force from the early part of the dream all around me. I wonder if it was me that was somehow born. I wake up. This dream was very frightening and I was afraid to go back to sleep because I might go back into the dream. I got out of bed and Wendy woke up. I told her about the dream. Over the years, I had forgotten about this dream except that I had a nightmare in which I was torn apart. As I reflect on this dream thirty years after it visited me, I think it might have served what Jung called a prospective function, in which the unconscious anticipates possibilities for the future somewhat like a rough draft or sketch.

The dream begins with my being called to evaluate children. This is nothing unusual, as I was a psychologist working with children and adolescents. I had been interested in parapsychology since my undergraduate college days, but had not really thought about this for many years. The rest of the dream imagery certainly harmonized symbolically with what would soon come into my life. Two months after the dream, Wendy and I would begin to study qigong with Master Mark. A university library is a place of knowledge and wisdom. Needing help from the custodian foreshadowed new teachers and guides who would help me open doors to new knowledge. Being torn apart by vines was a classic dismemberment dream written about by anthropologists who study traditional healers and shaman. I do not consider myself a shaman, but I was called to be a modern-day healer as both a psychotherapist and priest. My life certainly followed the traditional path of those called to this path in many traditional cultures.

I had a childhood near-death experience, followed by a dismemberment nightmare as an adult. While I did not know it at the time, these dreams are considered to be initiatory experiences. The woman in the ruined temple was a mentor or goddess with magical powers. Showing me how to use my hands to manipulate energy was something I would soon learn to do in qigong. Dreaming that I was a doctor helping a woman deliver her baby, foreshadowed the direction my counseling would evolve into, helping people to give birth to a new life. In my dream, my wondering whether the newborn baby was me was a foreshadowing of my own symbolic rebirth as healer and priest.

In order to become more aware of dreams and their meaning, the first step is asking for help from the Divine, the spirit world, or from your wisdom within. It's difficult to hear these messages if we are distracted by the noise from our electronic world. Turn off the radio or stereo. Turn off the television. Spend time away from social media and the news. Spend more time in silence, in the natural world, or in meditation. If Wendy hadn't taken some quiet time to ask for help at our altar, those olive oil bottles may still be in the closet behind the Navaho rug.

Everyone has about between four and six dreams each night. Some people remember most of their dreams and other say they never remember them. To remember your dreams and be able to mine the gold that is buried there, put a pen or pencil and a notepad on the nightstand next to you before you go to sleep. When you go to bed, tell yourself or pray that you will remember your dreams. As soon as you awaken, write down anything you remember, even if it is just a couple of images. Once you get in the habit of writing down your dreams, you will likely remember more details and more dreams. Just maybe a helpful spirit will appear in your dreams or even in a semi-dream state to help you. There is a line in the song, "Rainbow Connection" by Paul Williams, that always moves me to tears when I hear it.

## Chapter Nine: Spirits, Ghosts, and Dreams

*Have you been half asleep and have you heard voices? I've heard them calling my name. Are these the sweet sounds that called the young sailors, I think they're one and the same. I've heard it too many times to ignore it, there's something that I'm supposed to be. Someday we'll find it, the rainbow connection, the lovers, the dreamers and me.*

# Chapter Ten

# *Synchronicity*

We do not create our destiny; we participate in its unfolding.
Synchronicity works as a catalyst toward the working out of that destiny.
David Richo
The Power of Coincidence

In the course of our lives, most of us have said something to the effect of "What a strange coincidence." Almost everyone has experienced some type of coincidence in which two or more seemingly independent events, that have no apparent logical or causal connection, have a surprising, or very personally meaningful linkage. Our ancestors may have called them signs or omens. We think of a coincidence as an event that happens purely by chance, at random, and without any cause and effect involved. Richard Tarnas, the founding director of the graduate program in Philosophy, Cosmology and Consciousness at the California Institute of Integral Studies disagrees. He wrote in his book, *Cosmos and Psyche: Intimations of a New World View*, that sometimes, "The patterning can strike one as so extraordinary that it is difficult to believe the coincidence has been produced by chance alone. The events give the distinct impression of having been precisely arranged, invisibly orchestrated," (50). Some individuals I know would say that eagles flying above the medicine wheel dedication at Wendy's school was a coincidence, but given the spiritual significance that eagles have for the indigenous people in North America, this event had a powerful meaning to most of those present. Speaking and writing about meaningful coincidences, such as this, C. G. Jung gave them the name synchronicity. He was fascinated by these events, that while not related to each other in a cause-and-effect manner, seem to be manifestations of a type of orderliness in nature itself, but an orderliness that seems to transcend space and time as science understands it at the current time.

One Saturday, I was asked to come to a friend's home who had just found out she had a reoccurrence of cancer that had been in remission for several years. She was understandably scared and worried. We sat together and talked, with me mostly listening and asking an occasional question. I asked her if she would like me to use some external qigong to help with her anxiety and fear. She was very willing and eager to accept my offer, as she was familiar with qigong and had attended some of my qigong classes in the past. While I was sending qi, in what Master Hong calls, a qigong state, a very relaxed and focused state to open myself to the universal qi or healing energy, a very clear image or vision came into my mind, that seemed totally unrelated to what I was doing. I saw the altar in our home chapel. On it were two new tall votive candles, or *veladoras*, the kind I'd seen in Mexican grocery stores. On one was an image of Our Lady of Guadalupe and the other an image of Saint Martin de Porres. We had nothing like that on our altar. For those of you who are unfamiliar, Our Lady of Guadalupe is considered the patron saint of the Americas. She appeared as an apparition on a hill outside of Mexico City in December of 1531 to Juan Diego Cuauhtlatoatzin. She spoke to him in an Aztec dialect and her attire was reminiscent of the Aztec Earth Goddess, Tonantzin. Diego's Aztec name, Cuauhtlatoatzin, means 'talking eagle'. This was certainly synchronistic for me given my previous experience with eagles circling at Wendy's school and the encounter with Master Mark's Golden Eagle Spirit during my shengong apprenticeship, and with Elmer Running's Spotted Eagle spirit. In addition to those encounters, one day Wendy and I found a large feather on our deck. We didn't recognize it, so we brought it to a local state park to see if someone could identify it. One of the naturalists recognized it immediately as an eagle feather. Knowing that it was illegal

## Chapter Ten: Synchronicity

for non-indigenous people to have an eagle feather, we took it to a Lakota elder, who told us it was a gift from the eagle and we were meant to keep it. It is now on the altar in our home chapel and we use it for smudging with incense. The other image in my vision, Martin of Porres, was the seventeenth century son of a Spanish conquistador and a freed African slave. He was trained as a barber/surgeon and indigenous healer. He became the first lay Dominican brother of African descent, and because of his training, was placed in charge of the infirmary at the Dominican Monastery of the Holy Rosary in Lima Peru. He became known for his miraculous healings and it was said that injured or ill animals would find their way to the monastery for Brother Martin to heal them.

After I finished the qigong treatment, we ended our time together with the sacrament of the anointing of the sick. My friend's cancer did go back into remission, and while I do not take credit for this, her treatment is a good example of combining Western medicine with qigong healing and the sacraments. I want to note that it is very difficult to conduct Western style medical research to examine the efficacy of wholistic healing approaches. The reductionist methodology employed in Western scientific and medical studies are very difficult to set up to evaluate non-traditional healing because they cannot take into account all of the many and diverse variables involved in wholistic healing that are unique in each individual situation.

The day after visiting with our friend, Wendy and I went for a Sunday morning walk at Willow River State Park near our home. I was looking for a natural location to hold a retreat I was conducting what is called Into the Woods that would incorporate aspects of Japanese *shinrin-yoku*, or forest bathing, qigong, and end with a Holy Liturgy in the forest. We decided to walk the trail along the river just downstream from Little Falls Dam. As we made our way down the path, we heard rhythmic Latin music up ahead, and assumed people were enjoying a Sunday at the park down by the river bank and swimming in the river. As we continued walking, the music got louder and we could see a group of young Spanish speaking adults standing near and in the water. As we drew closer, we could see that they had turned a section of the rocky river embankment into a breathtakingly beautiful natural altar. About five feet of the rocky shoreline was covered with a variety of fruits, vegetables, wrapped candy, tobacco. There were small melons and mangos cut in half, hollowed out, and holding small burning candles. A piece of charcoal was burning on a flat rock and the sweet smell of copal incense coming from it drifted by on the light breeze. There was also a statue of the Blessed Virgin, about a foot and a half tall and dressed in homemade ornate cloth garments, standing on one of the rocks.

As we looked toward the river, we could see a few men in the swiftly flowing shallow water washing themselves off by pouring buckets of water over each other's backs and heads. Sitting on a large flat rock protruding from the water was an older woman wearing a bright yellow blouse with her hair wrapped in cloth the same yellow color. A younger woman was sitting in front of her, leaning against her. The woman in yellow was scrubbing her body with what we later discovered was a mixture of corn and cut up fruits. The older woman's assistant would occasionally dump a bucket of water over her to wash the mixture off.

Wendy asked a woman from the group who was standing next to us if it was okay to watch. She answered, "Of course." We each commented on the beauty of the river bank altar and the woman smiled and seemed pleased. Wendy asked if the older woman in the river was a healer. She answered, "Yes, Angela is a healer and more than that." She told us that all of the other people there were Angela's students. We both expressed what an honor it was for us to be there. The woman then asked Wendy if she would like to go into the river and participate. Wendy, who is much more spontaneous and extroverted than I am, excitedly agreed and asked me to hold her cell phone. She went down the embankment, took off her shoes, and walked into the river. She was greeted by a couple of young women and was guided through the strong current to a rock just in front of Angela and helped to sit down on it with her back leaning against the older woman like a child leaning against her mother's chest, being enfolded in her arms. Angela rubbed the mixture all over Wendy's arms, legs, neck, face, hair, and under her blouse both back and front. The helpers would rinse her off occasionally with buckets of river water. Angela then gave Wendy something to eat out of her hand.

As I watched, I noticed one of the men in the river pointing towards where I was standing with the woman who invited Wendy to participate. He began making beckoning hand gestures to join them in the river. I assumed this was intended for her, so I pointed to her. The man shook his head no and pointed at me again, gesturing for me to come and join them. Now that Wendy had participated, I knew I should overcome my introverted nature and experience this "dance" also. I gingerly went down the embankment, took off my hat and emptied the contents of my pockets into it. As I was taking off my shirt, a drenched Wendy, came out of the water, touched my back, and said joyfully, "Oh good! You're going in too." I smiled at her and stepped into the cool swift river water and was joined by two young men, one on either side of me, gently holding my arms at the elbows and escorting me to the rock in front of Angela. As I approached, she made the sign of the cross on herself and I reciprocated, making the sign of the cross also. As soon as I sat down on the rock, I could feel her strong hands rubbing her special mixture on my back and then, as with Wendy, on my arms, chest, neck, legs, head and face. One young man would occasionally dump a bucket of water over me with the warning, "Más agua en la cabeza," (more water on the head), before dumping it. It was as if the buckets of water washed all of my stress and worries out of my body and into the river where the current took it downstream and dissolved it. One of the young men asked me to cup my hands, and when I did, he put a piece of mango in them telling me to eat it, which I did. Angela spoke only Spanish, but one of her students translated her words to me. She said she saw a black man and a woman on my path who wanted to help me. When she was finished, I was escorted back to the river bank, where another man told me to cup my hands again. He poured oil into them, telling me to rub it all over my body, including in my hair and on my face as he was doing. The oil had the pleasant scent of cinnamon and other spices and it tingled on my skin as I rubbed it on. I must have been the last person to sit with Angela, because she got out of the river soon after I did, helped by two of her students. When she was comfortably on the river bank, another student handed her a bottle of beer. She took a sip from the bottle, then covered the top with her thumb and shook it. She then sprayed it on everyone again making the sign of the cross with the bottle. The bottle was then passed around, and we all took a sip of beer from it. It was a very spiritual beer communion. As we were gathering our belongings, Wendy asked if we should leave some money for Angela. The young man we asked, said, "No. just toss three pennies into the river in thanksgiving." We did this the next day, creating a little ritual of gratitude.

Soaking wet, we went back to our car and headed home to shower and change into dry clothes. On the way, Wendy kept touching her necklace, a pendent she had purchased in Glastonbury England at the Chalice Well Shop. The design was a *vesica piscis*, an ancient symbol of the divine feminine and the joining together of the visible and invisible worlds. This design appears in several places in the Chalice Well Gardens and was fabricated of wrought iron over wood as the cover of the well itself. Variations of this vesica piscis design can also be seen on many medieval European Catholic churches and on icons and religious painting from the medieval and renaissance periods. After a few minutes, Wendy looked over at me and said, "I feel like I have to give this to Angela. Let's go home and change and hopefully when we get back to the park, she will still be there." As soon as

## Chapter Ten: Synchronicity

we arrived home, we quickly changed into dry clothes and headed back to the park, which is only about four miles from our home. When we arrived, we saw that the group was still there having a picnic under the big pavilion nearest the river. One of the men with whom we had spoken earlier, was cooking chicken on the large grill. We asked him if we could speak with Angela. He told us to wait there and he would tell her that we wished to speak with her. As the young man spoke with her, she looked over at us, got up, and with another woman, came over to where we were standing. Wendy told Angela that she felt as if she had to give her the pendent. The other woman translated. Wendy explained its meaning. Angela nodded her head and told Wendy to fasten it around her neck. While Wendy was doing this, Angela asked her name. When Angela heard the name Wendy, she breathed in sharply in surprise and shock and looked as if she might faint. Her student held her up and explained that Angela's daughter, whose name is Wendy had recently died. Angela turned and hugged Wendy with tears in her eyes. Wendy later said that it was as if Angela's departed daughter had briefly come back through her, to give her mother a gift and a hug. After an appropriate time had passed, I told Angela about my vision the day before and asked her what she thought it might mean. She nodded her head smiling, and said San Martin de Porres was the black man, and Our Lady of Guadalupe was the woman she saw on my path, but she didn't say their names because she didn't know whether I would know who they were. Then she touched my arm, closed her eyes for a moment, opened them again and said, "Your healing work is to bring peace to those who come to you." My vision and our meeting with Angela seemed far more than a coincidence. She invited us to join them for the picnic, but not wanting to intrude, we went back home. This whole series of events was filled with synchronicity and perhaps some spirits were at work here too.

During the summer of 2011, a compelling series of synchronistic experiences occurred in my life. One evening, Wendy and I were discussing and wondering whether any particular archetypal or spiritual energies were helping me with my work as a psychotherapist, priest, and qigong healer, besides Our Lady of Guadalupe and St. Martin of Porres. At Wendy's suggestion, I went into our home chapel, lit incense, and then sat and meditated, asking if any spiritual helpers would identify themselves to me. That night I had the following dream: Wendy and I are outside and see a bear coming towards us in the distance. People start leaving the area. The bear comes right up and rubs against us. We are scared, but end up petting the bear on the neck and head. The dream shifts and we are with an old Native American man who tells us we must create a ceremony to honor the bear spirit.

In the morning, I shared this dream with Wendy and she was certain that the bear spirit or archetype had revealed itself in my dream. I was not convinced however, thinking this was probably just a coincidence. Later that afternoon we decided to go to the local cinema and see the movie *The Help*. Just before the movie began, when the screen was blank, the word bear, in very large print, moved across the screen. We turned and looked at each other in surprise. During the movie there was a subtle scene in which one of the characters is using a feather duster to clean a large bear taxidermy mount. We turned again, looking at each other in even greater surprise. After the movie, we decided to go for a walk out on the dike that goes out into the St. Croix River in our small town. As we walked, we noticed that there was a sailboat we hadn't seen before anchored just off the dike. When we passed by its stern, we saw that it was named Solar Bear. We were both astonished regarding these coincidences that had appeared one after the other. But it wasn't' over yet. The next morning, our son Andrew called to tell us that their dog woke them up in the middle of the night barking at a bear trying to get into a neighbor's garage. The culmination of this series of events happened later that afternoon. While I was cleaning and reorganizing my office, I picked up one of my old journals. I opened

## Chapter Ten: Synchronicity

it randomly and it fell open to a dream that I had the night before one of Wendy's birthday celebrations several years before. It was a dream I did not remember. Part of the birthday celebration involved Wendy moving around a medicine wheel I created in our back yard. Here is the dream as recorded in my journal:

> We are all gathered around the medicine wheel when a black bear comes out of the woods to the circle. I shout and wave my hands trying to chase it away, but it just growls at me and stays. We continued with the ceremony and the bear stays until the ceremony is over and then it wanders back into the woods.

This series of events and dreams had deep meaning for me. For me, the multiple appearances of the bear archetype in dreams and in waking life was clearly an answer to my meditational invitation. Over the years, I have had many more dreams in which a bear is a prominent archetypal image. I have also discovered that to both my Hungarian and Danish ancestors the bear was a healer and warrior spirit. Because they hibernate in winter, bears are the keepers of dreams, storing the wisdom of the dreams until the dreamer is able to understand them. Additionally, bear spirit understands the connection between the visible and invisible worlds and between the conscious and unconscious. My history as a martial artist, as a healer, vivid dreamer and dream worker make the bear archetype a quintessential spirit helper.

Sometime later, there appeared another bear dream that turned out to be significant. In this dream, I see a bear cub up in a tree. The branch of the tree is bending down with the bear's weight and the little bear is now close to me, so I take the cub from the tree and hold it against my chest. I hear a loud voice saying, "Gabriel—Faith." I think, *who are they?* I hear the voice again, "Gabriel—Faith. Don't forget." Then the dream ends. The next morning, I thought about the dream and remembered that Gabriel is the archangel whose Hebrew name means Messenger of God. It is traditionally the Angel Gabriel who appeared to Mary and to Mohammed. Faith, I realized, was not a person, but the message. Later that day, I saw my friend Kari and she told me that her last CT scan was not good and there are no more medical options she can try to treat her cancer. Then she said, "All that is left is faith." Faith—synchronicity from last night's dream. I offered to help her in any way she would like. A few months later, Kari had to be admitted into the hospital for surgery. I went along to pray with her and her family, and to anoint her with the sacrament of the sick. That night, I had the following dream: Kari is being harassed by a scary man. Suddenly a bear comes out of the woods and chases the man away. The bear wraps its arms around her and they fall to the ground, the bear covering her. I rush over thinking I must save her. As I draw near, the bear turns and looks at me, and I know it is not trying to hurt her but to protect her. I shared this dream with Kari, and she told me that the Native American healer with whom she had studied, was a member of the Bear Clan.

Sometimes our dreams work in conjunction with a waking experience as synchronicity. Jung explained that this manifests when there is a coincidence between a psychic state, like a dream, with an objective, external event, where there is no evidence of a causal connection between the two. I had a dream in which I was walking with Master Kwan, the abbot of the Shaolin Temple in the old Kung Fu TV series. The music from the television show was playing in the background of my dream. We are walking together through a large watermelon field and come to a picnic table. People are sitting at the table eating watermelon. We sit down at the table and join them. Master Kwan says to me, "Watermelon is good for your arthritis. Go on a three day fast eating only watermelon. This will purify your kidney qi." The next day, on my way home from a workshop led by James Gordon, MD, I stopped at a local bookstore and purchased a copy of his book, *Manifesto for a New Medicine*. That evening I started reading it. In the introduction, Dr. Gordon tells a story about seeing a client with arthritis. He tells the guy to go on a fast, eating only watermelon because it cleanses the kidneys. The next time I saw Master Hong, I told him that I had dreamed I was walking through a watermelon field with a Chinese sage who told me to eat watermelon. Then I asked him, "Should I trust these dreams?" Master Hong replied, "Your dream is good. Watermelon is cooling and gets heat out of the heart as well as good for the kidneys. Both are good for you. As you advance in your qigong skill, you will have dreams in which spirits will tell you how to treat the people who have come to you for help. This is very good."

Carl Jung and theoretical physicist, Wolfgang Pauli, came to the mutual conclusion that the human psyche and the world of physical matter were much more interwoven than the majority of scientific thought of their day had conceived. This idea led them to begin using the Latin term, *unus mundus* or "one world" to describe this and Jung theorized this connection was that which made synchronicity possible. Joseph Campbell suggested that when one follows their bliss by allowing themselves to be guided by an inner wisdom rather than by societal values, an unseen intelligence works to bring awareness to synchronistic experiences that lead them further along the path of individuation and theosis. Campbell points out that this unseen wisdom or Self, as Jung called it, seems to affect events regardless of time and distance. Jung also observed in his psychoanalytic work, that synchronicity played a recurrent theme in the lives of his clients during times of crisis, and of psychological and spiritual breakthrough. He also noted that they often occurred in a series of linked events, as in the case of my series of "bear" dreams and experiences, and in my repeatedly being called up to dance with indigenous people.

Synchronicity can open the door to the discovery of one's life purpose and meaning. In his autobiography, *Memories, Dreams, Reflections,* Jung revealed that many of his own synchronistic experiences inspired him to pursue his interest in understanding the deeper and more spiritual components and workings of the human psyche. Psychiatrist Jean Shinoda Bolen also shared with readers in her book, *The Tao of Psychology: Synchronicity and the Self*, that it was a series of synchronistic events in her life that led her to pursue a study of psychology (Mackey 21). As I have shared, synchronicity has also led me to explore and manifest new directions in my professional and personal growth.

Victor White, a Roman Catholic priest who corresponded and sometimes collaborated with Jung, believed that synchronistic events originate from the Holy Spirit, or God's presence, residing within, calling each person to wholeness. For Jung, synchronicity can guide us on the path to individuation which is at the very heart of his analytical psychology. Through the individuation process, one's psyche becomes fully integrated. But individuation is seen only as a way station on the journey to what Eastern Christianity calls theosis. According to Anthony Coniaris, Orthodox priest, scholar of religion, and psychiatrist, theosis is "the never-ending flowering of the image of God in us," (6). This is very similar to the Taoist teaching of the *Secret of the Golden Flower*, the Chinese text translated into German by Richard Wilhelm, a friend of Carl Jung, who wrote a commentary on it. Jung's insights into synchronicity offer the possibility of giving each and every one of us, the opportunity to discern the hints and nudges from the Spirit, on the journey to wholeness and theosis. On the stone above the entry door of his home on Lake Zurich in Küsnacht, Switzerland, Jung had chiseled the Latin inscription, *Vocatus Atque Non Vocatus Deus Aderit*, (Bidden or Unbidden, God is Present). This saying was also engraved on the headstone of Jung's grave.

In the classical Greek world, there were two ways of thinking about time. One classification of time was called *chronos*, in which time is perceived as sequential, linear and ordered, as we usually think of it regarding the year, month, day, and minutes of day-to-day activity. Chronos time is what we assume when someone asks, "What time is it?" or "When is your birthday?" But ancient Greek thinking also included what was referred to as *kairos* time. Kairos time is more enigmatic, more mysterious. Matthew T. Segall, who teaches philosophy, cosmology, and consciousness at the California Institute of Integral Studies states, "Kaironic time is full of potential... Kairos reveals to us that there are certain times when the order of things, the cosmos, the world-soul, is attempting to persuade we human souls to participate in the unfolding of events in a particular way," (Minding time). Perhaps synchronicity involves a shift from chronos to kairos time. Carl Jung, during the last few years of his life, began to think of synchronicity as an experience through which individuals could learn that there is a dynamic force in the universe, and that synchronicity is a manifestation of that force to nurture the individuation process and spiritual growth.

Perhaps the fictional *X-Files* television series character, FBI Agent Fox Mulder, is correct in his thesis that we are not alone. In moments of synchronicity, or in a series of synchronistic events, instead of feeling alone, or as separate and isolated entities in a vast universe, we feel an unseen connection at a deep and meaningful level. We feel connected to our ancestors, the spiritual realm, to the Eternal Tao, the Holy One, or a Cosmic Intelligence, and synchronicity gives us a very personal experience of the mystery.

# Chapter Eleven

# *The Three Paths Converge*

*The fates are toying with us now,
setting our feet on seemingly divergent paths
that still somehow converge in the most unlikely of places.*
Jonathon Randall, Outlander Season 2 Episode 5
*The cave you fear to enter
holds the treasure that you seek.*
Joseph Campbell, Reflections of the Art of Living

During one of my visits with Master Hong, I asked him if he would teach me specific qigong methods for treating chronic pain and life-threatening illness. He responded that he could do this, but then said something that befuddled me. He told me that some qigong healers are meant to help people with the final healing. A bit confused, I asked what he meant. He said some healers are called to help people to cross over into the next world when the time came. I responded that I did not want to work with people who were dying. He just smiled, patted me on the shoulder, and walked away to get a cup of green tea. I had absolutely no interest or desire to work with people who were dying. When I had my near-death experience as a child, I was basically unaware that I had been brought back from the threshold of death, and even thought my father, mother, and brother all died within a two-year period, I was not present when they died. As a young man, I did not want to go to funerals. I would soon discover however, that like Master Hong had done, the Divine Trickster, sometimes just smiles and gently nudges us in the direction in which we are called to go.

According to Joseph Campbell, at some point along the journey, the hero must face a Supreme Ordeal, confronting and overcoming their greatest challenge or fear. As in the quote at the beginning of this chapter, Campbell taught that mythically, we may find treasure in the cave we fear to enter, This Ordeal almost always involves facing death either metaphorically or literally, and for me, the Ordeal was quite literal. After completing my Clinical Pastoral Education, I was offered a job at Woodwinds Hospital as a chaplain and credentialed there as a psychologist. On my very first day at my new job, I received a page indicating that I was needed urgently in the emergency department. When I arrived, I was met by the triage nurse who told me that someone had just arrived in an ambulance who had been in an automobile accident. I was asked to support the family members who were arriving, while the medical team worked with the patient. I felt very comfortable and well trained for this role. After sitting and talking with the family for a while, a nurse called me aside and told me that the doctor wanted to speak with me in the treatment room. I excused myself and followed her. Upon entering the treatment room, I immediately realized just how very serious the accident had been. I was not at all prepared for what I saw, and I'm sure my shock was apparent. The patient was obviously dead and there was blood on the linens and on some of the staff's scrubs. One of the nurses, noticing my shocked expression, asked if I was okay. I shook my head yes and responded that I would be fine in a moment. After taking a few deep breaths, I felt my body begin to relax and the tension and anxiety releasing. This was the first time I had ever seen a dead person except in an open coffin at a memorial service. This was indeed an Ordeal for me.

As the doctor was cleaning himself up, he said that he would go and tell the family that the patient had died, but asked me to go with him and stay there with them. Glancing around the tiny room, I could see that the emergency team were clearly troubled because they had not been

## Chapter Eleven: The Three Paths Converge

able to save this person. The staff continued cleaning up the room and the deceased, so that the family could come in to be with the man for a while if they wished. When the doctor was ready, we both went to the waiting area. In a compassionate but professional voice, he told the family what had happened and that their loved one had passed away. He then explained what they had tried to do to save him. After a pause, he said that someone would come back and tell them when they could come to the treatment room to spend some time with their relative, if they so desired. I did my best to be a support for the family, answering whatever questions I could and offering to bring them coffee, tea, or water. Mostly I just sat with them and listened, asking a few questions that seemed appropriate. After a short time, we were escorted back to the treatment room. Things looked clean and organized, a much different scene than I had witnessed a little while before. After what seemed like a suitable length of time, I asked them if they wanted me to say a prayer. They responded positively, so I spontaneously prayed, feeling a bit awkward at first. All of my education and training as a psychologist, priest, and chaplain had not fully prepared me for this moment.

During the rest of the time I worked at Woodwinds, I served in several ways. I visited patients in their hospital rooms and in pre-op before surgery. I prayed if they desired, although I would sometimes defer to the family matriarch or patriarch to lead in a prayer if they were present and willing. I welcomed and blessed new babies, which was always a joy. Occasionally, I was asked to do a mental health evaluation of a patient, and yes, I continued to respond to emergency department calls. I discovered that a patient dying in the emergency department, or during surgery, was usually very distressing for the medical team involved, so I began to offer critical incident stress debriefings for them after a patient died. I also organized and provided a regular Caring for Yourself workshop for hospital staff, addressing potential burnout and teaching simple stress management and qigong techniques. In addition, I facilitated regular grief groups for families of those who had died in the hospital, and cancer support groups. As a priest, I was sometimes asked to administer the Sacrament of Anointing of the Sick and Holy Communion. Once monthly, I officiated at a Sunday morning Holy Eucharist in the hospital chapel. As time went on, I was asked more frequently to sit with patients at the Cancer Care Infusion Center who were fearful about chemotherapy. With some of these patients, I would simply sit and chat to distract them from what was going on. With others, I would teach simple qigong breathing to help them relax or combine qigong breathing with clinical hypnosis to help relieve their anxiety and fear. Some individuals would ask me to pray with them and I would often bless the medicine before it was started through the IV tube. I got to know the oncology staff and a couple of the oncologists well enough that they would ask me to join them when a family was about to hear an inauspicious diagnosis.

It became clear that the three paths of my hero's journey, had joined together. I was combining psychotherapy, qigong, and spiritual care with individuals and groups. Over time, I became more and more comfortable working with the dying and with death, and I saw my work as a paradox. It was both a wonderful and a terrible vocation. And when I use the term vocation, I mean it in its original Latin sense as a calling. I began to see my work with the dying and the dead as an honor. Always having loved and finding comfort in rituals, I developed one for those who died at the hospital—most likely borrowed from something I'd read. I would begin by lighting a candle (actually turning on a battery operated one because flames weren't permitted in the hospital rooms). I would bring a pan of warm water, some washcloths and a towel into the deceased person's room. Then, I would begin to lovingly and gently wash the deceased person's face, neck, arms, hands, legs and feet, while saying a prayer of thanks for each body part that had served them and their family during their life.

## Chapter Eleven: The Three Paths Converge

After a short time, I would ask if any of the family members present would like to join me in this washing ritual. Some did, others did not. Sometimes a family member would spontaneously begin to comb the person's hair or put makeup on a deceased woman. Years later, when Wendy's mother passed away, she spontaneously did this for her. Washing her, changing her clothes, brushing her hair and putting makeup on her mom was a beautiful, meaningful, and impactful ritual for Wendy, me, and for her mother's spirit.

Spirits, ghosts, and dreams also played a role in this area of working with the dying and deceased. It was common for people who were very near death to tell me that they saw a deceased loved one, either in a dream or in their room, to guide them into the next realm. The first time this happened, a woman said that her husband was in the room. Not seeing anyone, and as a rookie chaplain, I asked her where he was. She responded, a bit irritated, "He is standing right next to you Father," pointing to my right side. I turned my head to the right and said that I was glad he could be with us. Later that day, a nurse told me that her husband had died a couple of years before.

My role as a spiritual companion to my friend Kari is a treasured experience of the ordeal of facing the death of another, and in her case, a dear friend. As her cancer progressed, we both knew she would die soon. I had been visiting with her almost daily and had anointed her. One night, Wendy had a moving archetypal dream. In her dream, Kari was standing on the bank of a stream. I was standing in the middle of the stream on a rock, and on the opposite bank was Saint Martin de Porres. The three of us were holding hands and we were helping Kari to cross over to the other side of the stream. Wendy told me that she thought the dream was revealing an important part of my role in helping others and I remembered what Master Hong had told me that being a qigong healer sometimes meant helping people to cross over into the next world when the time came. After helping

Kari "unhook the latches" from her dream, she told me that she knew all of the latches were open. She thanked me for all I had done to help her physically and spiritually. A couple of days later, I received a phone call from Kari's sister telling me that she had passed away. I was in Duluth at the time and felt very sad that I was not with her when she departed.

As time passed, the brokenhearted with whom I worked, both at the hospital and in private practice, became almost exclusively individuals who were dealing with cancer or other life-threatening or chronic diseases I occasionally counseled family members who were grieving the loss of a counselee who had died from one of these illnesses. As I became more comfortable and skilled using my integrative approach, I also began to examine my methods from a more academic framework, and finally, confronting the unfinished business of not completing my doctorate at the University of Minnesota those many years before, I completed a doctoral program in transpersonal counseling and wrote my PhD dissertation in which I presented a theoretical argument for the validation and benefits of the integrated approach to transpersonal counseling which I had developed.

While my approach proved unique enough to be accepted for my dissertation topic, it is really nothing new. In fact, early in our human history, tribal healers included prayer, song, sacred ritual, herbs, and touch to restore the health of members of their tribe. We don't really know when our ancestors began incorporating the mind of the afflicted person in healing, although in his 1922 edition of, *The Golden Bough*, James George Frazer surmised from his study of religion, magic, and science, that our ancient ancestors probably suspected that bodily illnesses were somehow related to the mind very early on. With Descartes' division of science and religion, mind and body however, there was less and less room for the heretofore held view of a connected, holistic universe, and an increasingly reductionist approach to medicine. This clear-cut separation continues for some physicians who practice in the Western world. Change, however, began to slowly occur during the cultural revolution of the 1960s, sparking a renewed interest and demand for complementary and alternative medicine (CAM) as well as the growth of the transpersonal psychotherapy movement. More and more hospitals in the United States now offer some form of CAM therapy, and more and more medical schools are offering classes on CAM in their curricula. When I worked at Woodwinds Hospital, patients were offered acupuncture, healing touch, and aromatherapy as complements to the allopathic medical treatment they received.

Jungian analyst and Episcopalian priest, John A. Sanford maintained that we may better understand illness if we understand what health means, beyond the functioning of our mechanical and chemical body. Sanford pointed out that the word health comes from the old Saxon word *hal*, which is the root of the words hale and whole. Wholeness implies all aspects of the person functioning harmoniously. A holistic approach is immensely important for the individuals with whom I work. Integrative oncologist Jeremy Geffen, MD, expressed in his book, *The Journey Through Cancer*, that while cancer patients' biological indicators and symptoms are conscientiously monitored, other important areas of their life are virtually ignored by the medical profession. Dr. Geffen became convinced that it is vital to help patients emotionally and spiritually and assist them in experiencing a sense of peace. There it is again, that word "peace," the calling Angela told me was mine, that day on the Willow River.

Kelly A. Turner, PhD, agrees with Geffen. She interviewed individuals who had experienced a radical remission of their cancer and published her results in the book, *Radical Remission: Surviving Cancer Against All Odds*. She defined radical remission as the disappearance of an individual's cancer that was "statistically unexpected." Dr. Turner discovered that all of those who experienced a radical remission had employed a holistic treatment approach to their illness. Drs. Turner and Geffen emphasize the importance of patients seeking the best medical care available and embracing a healthy diet as part of their cancer treatment, but the other areas they have shown to be important are not the bailiwick of the typical medical doctor. They include: social support, releasing and healing emotions, utilizing the power of the mind to tap into the body's natural healing capacity, finding a meaning and a purpose to live for, and developing a spiritual connection that can be thought of as God, the Tao, a sense of oneness, or love.

While their research was limited to people with cancer, we can logically assume that applying the same holistic approach to people who are dealing with other life threatening and chronic diseases would also benefit from them. After reading their books, I realized that I was already incorporating many of these ideas in my integrative counseling. I encourage individuals and group members to seek out the best possible medical care and to work with a nutritional professional for dietary advice. I offer them emotional support through groups or in individual counseling sessions. In our work together, we address the stress and fear that comes with a diagnosis of a serious disease and we work together to find methods they can use to reduce or cope with their pain and the unpleasant side effects of chemotherapy or medication. We also address any unconscious emotional complications, allowing for the exploration of their personal spirituality and meaning. The individuals with whom I work, often report that in retrospect, their medical diagnosis was an existential crisis. It acted as the triggering event that started them on their own hero's journey and led them on a path of personal and spiritual transformation. For others, their initial diagnosis of a life-threatening disease led to despondency and a sense of meaninglessness. Their diagnosis began their own Supreme Ordeal. My role is to accompany these brokenhearted individuals and guide them through the darkness and fear to find their inner wisdom and healing. I found that as I utilized my integrative approach to counseling more and more, I identified

## Chapter Eleven: The Three Paths Converge

with Dr. Gerald May as articulated in his book, *The Dark Night of the Soul: A Psychiatrist Explores the Connection Between Darkness and Spiritual Growth*. He wrote:

> All too often though, our preoccupation with finding relief left little opportunity to look for meaning. This is the curse of the health-care system dedicated only to fixing problems, a system too streamlined to be concerned with what's happening to people's souls. Frustrated, I found myself gradually leaving the practice of medicine and dedicating myself more to the art of spiritual companionship. Here the priorities are reversed; we continue to care about easing suffering, but the meaning is what's most important (6).

My goal became to practice psychotherapy in the sense of its original meaning from the Greek: *therapeia*, to heal or minister, and *psyche*, the soul, mind, or spirit. To borrow from C. G. Jung, I discovered that, "The fact is that the approach to the numinous is the real therapy, and inasmuch as you attain to the numinous experience, you are released from the curse of pathology. Even the very disease takes on a numinous character" (Letters Vol. 1, Aug 31, 1945). Numinous, from the Latin *numen*, and *nuere*, literally means a divine beckoning. For Jung, it was not the content, but the mysterious quality of the numinous experience that was important and brought about some kind of healing to the person.

I began referring to myself as a pastoral counselor and joined the American Association of Pastoral Counselors (AAPC). This now seemed like a much better fit than practicing as a psychologist. Pastoral counselors have received graduate training in both religion or theology and the behavioral sciences. According to the AAPC, pastoral counseling is a form of psychotherapy that uses spiritual resources as well as psychological understanding for healing and growth. A central theme in pastoral counseling is an awareness of the transpersonal or spiritual dimension in human wholeness. In addition, I embraced the belief of Dr. William Glasser that love and belonging is our primary human need. I saw that the most important component of my role as a counselor was the relationship I developed with my counselees. Demonstrating genuine "compassionate love," defined as a love that combines empathy, kindness, consideration, as well as devotion and care, became a crucial aspect of the counseling journey.

The final and most dramatic manifestation of my Supreme Ordeal appeared only a few months after completing my doctorate. Wendy and I were looking forward to celebrating my accomplishment by driving down to Arizona to participate in the graduation ceremony in May and spend additional time hiking around Sedona and the Grand Canyon. But on March 15, a series of events set into motion what reminded me of Shakespeare's play, *Julius Caesar*, in which Caesar is warned by a soothsayer, "Beware the Ides of March." Wendy and I had been raking snow off of our roof from a March storm. When we finished, we decided to go to a local coffee cafe and relax. As I sat enjoying my coffee and reading, I began to experience a sharp pain in my left arm and in the left side of my chest by my arm pit. I assumed I had strained a muscle raking the snow, but it finally got painful enough that it became difficult to inhale deeply, so I asked Wendy to drive me to the emergency department at our local small Hospital. What I thought would be a quick evaluation, ended up taking four hours. After four EKGs and two blood tests, the emergency room doctor said that I had not had a heart attack, or at least there was no damage to my heart indicating that I had. He suggested however, that I make a follow-up appointment with my primary care physician in the next three days. I followed up as he recommended, and my primary care doctor said it probably was just a

## Chapter Eleven: The Three Paths Converge

pulled muscle, but just to be sure, and since both of my parents had died from cardiovascular events, I should have a stress echocardiogram. I was sure the test would turn up nothing. My blood pressure was controlled by a low dose of medication and my cholesterol level was not considered high. But unanticipatedly, my agreement to have this test, turned out to be like Neo's decision to take the red pill in the film, *The Matrix*, followed by Morpheus's comment, "All I'm offering is the truth, nothing more."

A few days later, I was walking faster and faster on a treadmill having a stress test, which surprisingly, I failed. This was followed by a CT angiogram, followed by a traditional angiogram. The angiogram revealed that I had a blockage in my left main coronary artery. The doctor told us that I would need coronary bypass surgery as soon as possible. I responded that I would schedule the surgery right after my graduation. He replied that the type of blockage I had, was often called the widow maker and air travel was not recommended. He continued saying I may well not make it home from my graduation and vacation. At home, Wendy and I talked it over and I decided that we would both be more comfortable having the surgery at Mayo Clinic. When I told the cardiac care secretary at Mayo my story, they scheduled my surgery for the next week. We were lucky to have a young friend who worked as a nurse in the cardiac recovery unit at Mayo Clinic Hospital, St. Mary's Campus. She reassured us of the skill of the surgeon, Dr. Rowse, and of the excellent quality of care given by the dedicated cardiac surgery recovery unit staff at Mayo's St. Mary's Hospital. On our first day at St. Mary's, we met with Dr. Rowse, who spent over an hour with us explaining exactly what he planned to do and showing us images from the echocardiogram, elucidating exactly why he had made his decisions. Dr. Rowse planned to use my mammary arteries and do a double bypass. He believed that this option should last for the rest of my, hopefully long, life. We left his office very pleased with our decision to have the surgery at Mayo. On our way back to our hotel room, we stopped at the St. Mary's chapel where, synchronistically, a priest was offering the Sacrament of the Anointing of the Sick. I participated along with three other people. It was a bit surreal to receive the sacrament that I had given to others so many times before, but it was very comforting.

The next morning, we checked in at the hospital as directed at 5:30 am, where we were greeted by my daughter Chrissie, who had driven there from Chicago to be with us. It was fitting that my daughter, whose fever as a toddler sent me on my hero's journey, was there as I faced this critical point, this Supreme Ordeal, on the journey. I was most grateful however, that she was there to be with Wendy throughout this frightening time. Because Chrissie is a registered nurse who has worked in hospital settings, she was able to answer our questions, and ask the staff the right questions while I was in the hospital for five days. I was then taken by myself to a small pre-op room where I was told to take off all of my clothes, even my wedding ring and put on the usual demeaning hospital gown with the opening in the front. Then a nurse came in and shaved the entire front on my body from my neck down to my ankles. The whole procedure reminded me of the myth of the Goddess Inanna's decent into the underworld. As Inanna passed through each of seven gates descending into the netherworld, she had to discard one of her garments until she arrived into the realm of the dead naked.

Wendy and Chrissie soon joined me again. The anesthesiologists stopped by to introduce themselves and tell me what they would do for anesthesia and a nurse placed an IV line in my arm. After a short time, I was wheeled down the hall toward the operating room. Wendy and Chrissie walked next to me for as long as they were allowed, and then we parted with kisses. Wendy later told me that as soon as I passed through those surgery area doors, she was overwhelmed with pent up emotions and wept on Chrissie's shoulder. As I continued on my way to the operating room, I realized that while I was not afraid of dying, I was not ready to leave this life. I wanted to stay with Wendy, my children, grandchildren, and my dear friends as long as possible. I began to pray silently the prayers of my childhood: the Memorare, the Our Father, the Hail Mary, and then spontaneous prayers for a successful surgery and that the surgical team would be guided by and receive help from the spiritual world. I prayed that the spirits and saints that I called upon to help others, would now help me. Once in the surgery room, I chatted with the anesthesiologists and then one of them placed an oxygen mask on my face and told me to breathe deeply, as if I were breathing into my toes. It made me smile to be told to use a method I had used many times with others, minus the mask, to help them reduce their anxiety. Then he told me that he was going to inject anesthesia drugs into my IV and I would fall asleep. I lost consciousness with the words of Julian of Norwich in my head, "All shall be well, and all shall be well, and all manner of thing shall be well."

Although the line between life and death has become more ambiguous as medical knowledge and science improves, the traditional, or mythic definition for death has always been when the heart stops beating on its own. During my open-heart surgery, Dr. Rowse made a ten-inch-long vertical incision in the middle of my chest and then cut my breastbone in half lengthwise, spreading it apart to expose my heart. I was then connected to a heart-lung bypass machine that pumped my blood throughout my body. My heart was stopped so that Dr. Rowse could operate on a still heart with no blood flowing through it. In one sense then, I was now dead. I had wondered whether I might have another near-death experience, but I did not, just darkness until waking up confused in the cardiac intensive care unit.

While I was in surgery, the team kept Wendy up to date through text messages. At one point, Wendy and Chrissie decided to walk down to the chapel, which is really a big old ornate Catholic Church to pray for me. They sat in one of the pews nearest to the front facing the altar. At some point Wendy said she was going to go somewhere, and Chrissie said she wanted to stay a little longer. While praying, Chrissie started reminiscing about sitting in church as a child, while I played the guitar and led the congregation in song. She especially remembered her favorite song, "On Eagles Wings," by Michael Joncas, but she couldn't remember all of the lyrics.

On the back of the pew in front of her was a closed box or rack. She opened it and inside there was a missal and several hymnals. She picked up one of the hymnals, opened it to a random page, and to her surprise the song "On Eagles Wings" appeared. This is another instance of synchronicity, but I would like to think it was the Divine One saying, "I am with you and with your dad and everything will turn out fine."

I don't really remember much of my first couple of hours in the Cardiac ICU except that when I was waking up, I felt I was choking, and someone removed my breathing tube, allowing me to breathe on my own again, a first breath after being mythically dead. The breath of life. Wendy and Chrissie told me later that the first thing I said was, "Oh! I'm still here." Chrissie responded to me by asking, "Did you think you were going to see Jesus?" I answered that I thought I might. After becoming more lucid, I realized there were now IV tubes in both wrists, in both arms, at the inside of my elbow joints, and one in my neck. There were also three drain tubes coming out of my torso: one under each breast and one in the center, just below my sternum. As the day turned into late night, Chrissie went to her hotel room to sleep. Wendy wanted to stay, but was talked into going back to her hotel room to get some sleep also, against her better judgment. The staff promised to notify her if there were any changes or problems, but somehow, that message did not find its way into the hands of the night shift.

As the darkness of night engulfed me, I began to feel like I was in an awake nightmare. Even though I occasionally ask counselees to do this, I have always been a bit skeptical of the idea of rating one's pain using a scale of one through ten, usually accompanied by a piece of paper with a series of annoying emoji faces, from smiling to very sad. I've never been sure about how to rate my own pain. That night however, I would have easily rated it a nine, and I say nine only if it was out of a high of ten where I would have passed out. Somehow, my medical records that were passed on to Mayo indicated that I was allergic to morphine and related narcotic pain medications. Now, it is true that I had experienced some nausea and a rash from morphine during a previous knee surgery, but this is a fairly common reaction for many people. I'm not sure what they did use for pain control, but whatever it was, it did not work very well at all. Then someone decided to try Ketamine. Ketamine is a dissociative anesthetic that has hallucinogenic effects. It is used to help people feel detached from their pain feeling more relaxed. Ketamine can induce a state of amnesia, resulting in no memory of what has happened. It can also cause immobility. My experience of this medication was like being in a Dantesque hell. I was still in pain but it was like watching myself from outside of my body and I was paralyzed. I had hallucinations, some of which were swirling colors, but most were frightening and I could not move to defend myself against my hallucinatory specters. When the ordeal was finally over, I did not experience amnesia. In fact, I remember that night all too well, and for a few months after the surgery, I occasionally had flash-backs as one does who has Post Traumatic Stress Disorder (PTSD).

Thankfully, Wendy returned just after sunrise and was told that I had a very bad night. She was angry that she had not been called. The nurse on duty told her that the difficulty was caused because I could not have any narcotics. Wendy asked to see the physician's assistant on duty, and told him that I was not allergic to morphine and insisted that they give me some type of narcotic pain medication. I was then given a very small dose of morphine and it brought a rapid reduction in pain. Since I had no allergic reactions to this dose, I was given a normal dose of morphine while I was in the hospital. This experience was indeed the Supreme Ordeal of my hero's journey and my goddess had helped me return from death and hell to resurrection. While the surgery was a complete success, the healing process from open-heart surgery is a long one. While the Supreme Ordeal is a necessary and crucial stage of the hero's journey, it is not the resolution or the end.

In Campbell's monomyth, the hero returns home and celebrates their survival of the Ordeal. The returning hero is not the same person who left on the journey and returns with some type of treasure, elixir, or wisdom to bestow on the community. The hero has journeyed from innocence to disenchantment to re-enchantment and now is prepared to help others find and navigate their own journey. Although I had missed my graduation, a more meaningful celebration took place in its stead. My children and grandchildren traveled to our home for a summer long weekend and put together a beautiful and meaningful ceremony for me. I had returned from my very long journey with the gift of an integrative transpersonal approach to counseling to help the brokenhearted find peace and wholeness. The journey had helped define my purpose in the world.

I had faced death and survived. The members of the cancer support group that I facilitate expressed it best. When I returned to the group after my heart surgery, they told me that while they had always appreciated and valued all that I brought to them, only now was I truly a member of the group. I was one of them because only now could I understand what it was like to face death, and because of that, I was a new person. A moment from the past flashed through my mind when they said this. The first time my young grandsons saw me in my monastic robes of the Lindisfarne Community, of which I am a professed member, their eyes opened wide, and they said excitedly, "Grampa, you're a Jedi." I guess, from an archetypal point of view, I now was.

# Chapter Twelve

# *One Thing*

"If one knows himself, he will know God,
and knowing God, will become like God"
Clement of Alexandria, The Instructor, Book 3

Along the three roads of my hero's journey, I had come to a point where it seemed I had finally reached an end to the quest. On my way, I had experienced many trials, I suffered, found love, learned many new skills, and grew emotionally, intellectually, and spiritually. I experienced death and rebirth and brought back the gift of integrative transpersonal counseling to help the brokenhearted and suffering among my fellow travelers. There was however, one more stage on Campbell's hero's journey with which I needed to wrestle. He calls this stage *apotheosis*, an ancient Greek term for gaining the insights of the gods and becoming godlike. Mythically, this usually occurs through some type of epiphany, insight, or revelation. Aristotle taught that not just humans, but everything is searching for its *telios*; its completeness or wholeness. The three paths of my hero's journey each have their own way of hypothesizing about this apotheosis.

American psychologist Abraham Maslow introduced his theory of the development of psychological needs in the 1940s. He believed that we humans, once our basic needs are met, have an inborn desire to become self-actualized. For most of his life he considered self-actualization to be the highest level of psychological development. It seems to me that self-actualization is humanistic psychology's equivalent to apotheosis. Those who are self-actualized have come to a full realization of their creative, intellectual, and interpersonal possibilities. Near the end of his life however, Maslow made an important, but little-known change to his theory. At the pinnacle of his hierarchy, above self-actualization, he added self-transcendence. He defined self-transcendence in his last book, *The Farther Reaches of Human Nature* as the "very highest and most inclusive or holistic levels of human consciousness, behaving and relating . . . to oneself, to significant others, to human beings in general, to other species, to nature, and to the cosmos," 269). Maslow considered mystical or numinous experiences to be a key. He wrote that self-transcendence included feelings of euphoria, wonder and awe, and a deep knowing that something extremely valuable had happened. The self-transcendent person is transformed in a way that positively effects their daily living. For Maslow, self-transcendence includes a spiritual awakening that frees the individual from the domination of the ego, and results in an awareness of the unity of all things.

In the Depth Psychology of Carl Jung, the term "Individuation" takes the place of apotheosis. Individuation is the process of self-realization in which we discover and experience meaning and purpose in life. Through individuation, we become whole. When Jesus says, in Matthew's gospel, "Be perfect, just as your Father in heaven is perfect" (5:48), the Greek word translated as perfect is *telios*, that completeness and wholeness of Aristotle. For Jung, this is accomplished by bringing the unconscious, both personal and transpersonal, into conscious awareness. In Jung's ideation, individuation means the realization of the Self, which is the archetype of wholeness described by Jungian analyst Frith Luton as the "transpersonal power that transcends the ego." Jung, in *Psychology and Religion,* called the Self "God within us" and stated that an encounter with the Self felt like a religious experience. The awareness and connection with the Self is a vital goal of the individuation process. Individuation occurs when the ego allows the Self to guide the way.

Before I continue however, I want to correct a misunderstanding. This does not mean somehow getting rid of the ego, as advocated by some, who I refer to as New Age teachers. That would neither be possible nor would it be desirable. Our ego is what organizes our thinking, memories, feelings and sensations. Without a strong and healthy ego, we would be overwhelmed by a never-ending flood of day-to-day sensory input, interactions, and decisions. In addition, the ego helps us to establish clear and strong boundaries that protect us from external threats from the world, as well as internal threats buried in the shadows of the unconscious, such as past trauma, until such time as we are able to deal with them. The ego however, does want to remain in firm control and resists the individuation process, which involves exploring those shadowy areas of the unconscious that the ego views as threatening. The Self, because of its transpersonal connection, has a perspective and knowledge that the ego alone cannot understand. Rather than dissolving the ego and dissolving oneself into God, Jung encouraged people to look for what the Self wants us to do in this world, for some purpose for which we are called. In his personal journal, known as *The Red Book*, Jung wrote, "What is important and meaningful to my life is that I shall live as fully as possible to fulfill the divine will within me (75).

Jung was admonished by some in both the psychological and religious communities for equating the Self with God. He, however, refuted this accusation, clearly stating that the Self was not God per se, but rather an archetype or representation of God within the psyche. In *Civilization in Transition*, he explained that the Self never takes the place of God, but may be a "vessel of divine grace." Jungian analyst Murray Stein argues that through the Self, the psychological and the religious come together in such a way that neither is diminished.

Apotheosis is often experienced as a direct encounter with the divine within and the spiritual realization that occurs when this encounter is validated and reinforced through the mind and the senses. Like any archetype, the Self, in its essence, is unknowable, but like all archetypes, it may appear symbolically in our dreams as a person, such as a mythic character of great power, an animal, or even a symbol such as a mandala or the heart. Archetypal dream images of the Self can generate both awe and fear because they are so powerful. The bears in my dreams could be an archetype of the Self. Because the Self is an integration of our personal and transpersonal psyche, it sometimes seems as though we know things that are beyond our conscious possibility of knowing, and our experiences of the Self are numinous or transcendent. These moments or encounters with the Self move us to further connect with that which is beyond the personal to the transpersonal.

In Eastern Orthodox Christianity, apotheosis is usually referred to as theosis or deification. The Eastern Church views salvation differently than the Western evangelical teaching of accepting Jesus as one's personal savior and being assured of going to heaven when we die. Salvation in the Eastern Church is theosis. It is a life-long process of healing and transformation leading toward union with the Divine. In his letter to the Philippians Saint Paul wrote, "Work out your salvation with fear and trembling. For the One working in you is God, both to will and to work for God's own good pleasure" (2:12-13). Theosis is following our holy calling to, as the Army advertising slogan says, "Be all that you can be." It is realizing our fullest potential, our calling, our vocation. Vocation is not the same as our career, although, if we are very lucky, the two can coincide. It is not something one chooses but something to which one is called. This is reflected in the Orthodox Holy Mystery (Sacrament) of Baptism. As a priest, I say during the rite, "You are baptized. You are illuminated. You are anointed with Holy Chrism. You are sanctified. You are washed in the name of the Father and the Son and the Holy Spirit. Become what you already are." This is the Eastern Christian understanding of the words of Jesus in the gospels, telling his listeners to be perfect, even as God is perfect, and "'You are gods." This is theosis.

## Chapter Twelve: One Thing

The path of qigong can also lead to apotheosis. In 1923, Carl Jung met Richard Wilhelm and that encounter began a lifelong friendship. Jung shared reminiscences of their affiliation in his *Memories, Dreams, Reflections*. They had many discussions on how Chinese philosophy could provide a deeper understanding of the unconscious. Jung also wrote commentaries on Wilhelm's translations of *The Secret of the Golden Flower* and *the I Ching*. Reflecting on his commentary, Jung remarked that his discussions with Wilhelm and the writing of these commentaries were instrumental in conceiving his concepts of the Self and Individuation. In a letter to Wilhelm, Jung described the role of their friendship as two pillars that support a bridge connecting the East and the West. *The Secret of the Golden Flower* is a Taoist text that metaphorically describes an inner psychological and spiritual journey, by means of qigong meditation, towards the Self. While Wilhelm defined the Golden Flower as a golden ball or the elixir of life, it is reminiscent of the pearl of great price of which Jesus spoke and the alchemical philosopher's stone. According to the *Secret of the Golden Flower*, the awakening of spiritual consciousness depends upon the shen. In Chinese qigong philosophy, the *shen*, translated as both mind and spirit, resides in the heart. The shen is what brings mental and spiritual awareness to the psyche. From a purely scientific perspective, brain and heart scan studies, carried out on qigong practitioners, have discovered that regular qigong practice increases coherence between the heart and brain. Kenneth Cohen, whose book, *The Way of Qigong*, first influenced me to combine psychotherapy and qigong healing, argues that one can infer from this coherence research that qigong practice may contribute to the development of "a harmonious and integrated sense of self" (66). His statement can easily refer to Jung's Self and the Individuation process.

Another embodiment of apotheosis appears in Janet Hagberg's wonderful book, *Real Power: Stages of Personal Power in Organizations*. I often mentally refer to the ideas presented in her book during a counseling session to help me understand a counselee's current experience of personal power. Hagberg defines personal power as emanating from both external sources such as educational degrees and training, and from inner resources acquired through introspection, life's struggles, and the realization and development of one's life purpose. Apotheosis coincides with the last stage Hagberg presents and names "Power by Gestalt." People at this stage are comfortable with the paradoxes of life and have integrated their shadows. They realize that mind, body, and spirit all work together. They are ethical, moral, and living a life of quiet service to their purpose. Individuals at this stage are no longer afraid of death.

When I reflect on this juncture of the hero's journey, a scene from the 1991 film, *City Slickers*, in which Curly, the old rugged cowboy, Mitch's sometimes frightening and wise mentor, shares his wisdom.

> Curly: Do you know what the secret of life is?
>
> Mitch  No. What?
>
> Curly: This. (Holding up his index finger)
>
> Mitch: our finger?
>
> Curly: One thing. Just one thing. You stick to that and everything else don't mean shit.
>
> Mitch: That's great, but what's the one thing?
>
> Curly: That's what you've got to figure out.

I remember having a few enjoyable philosophical discussions trying to figure out the "one thing," as if there was some universally correct answer. But I have come to think Curly was right. "That's what you've got to figure out." And the you to which Curly is referring, is you in the singular. It is the individual you. As Famous French writer Marcel Proust wrote in his book *Remembrance of Things Past*. "We don't receive wisdom; we must discover it for ourselves after a journey that no one can take for us or spare us." But I can share some thoughts that may help each of you discover your own "one thing." First of all, in spite of the mythology of the advertising gods, it is not about finding the right career that will bring you the most money, or fame, or status. It can only be found by following our calling, or true vocation. A vocation (from Latin call, summons) is work to which a person is singularly drawn, and for which they are particularly well suited. Campbell tells us that sometimes, "We must be willing to let go of the life we planned so as to have the life that is waiting for us." That life can be found by following what Campbell called your bliss. It seems that following one's bliss, corresponds with finding what you are truly passionate about and what gives you great joy. Your bliss is your life's purpose. American theologian Frederick Buechner said it is the place to which God calls us, where our "deep gladness and the world's deep hunger meet," (118-119) Wendy says, "Our heart's desire (our bliss) is the will of God." The challenge then, is discerning our true heart's desire from what society and advertisers tell us our desires should be.

One of the most famous Western myths of the hero's journey involves the search for the Holy Grail. One night I had a long dream that ended like this: I am in an open field in which some large colorful tents are set up. They remind me of the tents that medieval knights have as they are preparing for a joust in films. The night sky is clear and filled with stars. As I look around, I see that one of the tents is glowing from within. I walk to it, and as I open the flap to enter, I see a priest in elaborate gold vestments. He is behind an altar and holding up a chalice and I knew it was the Holy Grail. Angels are on either side of him. I only get a glance of the Grail when the dream ends.

In Christian mythology, the Holy Grail is the cup that Jesus used at the Last Supper. For Carl Jung, the Grail was the principle of individuation. Joseph Campbell considered the Holy Grail to be the pearl of great value spoken of by both Jesus and Lao Tzu. In the Gospel of Matthew, Jesus says: "The kingdom of heaven is like a merchant's search for fine pearls. When one of great value was found, the merchant went back and sold everything else and bought it" (13:45-46). Lao Tzu said, "The Tao is the sage's priceless pearl, and it redeems everything" (Tao te Ching 62). So, where do we find this valuable pearl —this Holy Grail that redeems everything and that someone would sell everything to obtain? Jesus teaches us in the Gospel of Luke that, "The kingdom of God is within you" (Luke 17:21). Lao Tzu says we "find the truth within" (Tao the Ching 5). So, it seems that the real search for the Grail is an inner search.

Renowned authority on mystical spiritual traditions, Richard Smoley, wrote, "The Grail is the heart, illumined and awakened so that it may serve as a receptacle for divine energies," (12). Russian Orthodox mystic Alexander Mumrikov taught that if seekers pray from the heart, a kind of interior grail can be felt opening upward and they can experience the transformation of the energy as it takes place. In Eastern Orthodoxy, the heart, like in qigong refers to the innermost core of the person, and as the psalmist wrote, we can hear what God will speak to us when we open our hearts. (85:8). This was the advice I was given by the healer from South America, to open my heart. French philosopher and mathematician Blaise Pascal while a strong advocate of reason, wrote, "The heart has reasons, which reason does not know. We feel it in a thousand things. It is the heart that feels God, and not reason" (Pensées, The Wager, p.5). The *Secret of the Golden Flower* teaches that while anyone can read the text, its wisdom can only be transmitted from heart to heart. Antoine de Saint-Exupéry, in his book, *The Little Prince* expressed this beautifully. "And now here is my secret, a very simple secret: It is only with the heart that one can see

## Chapter Twelve: One Thing

rightly; what is essential is invisible to the eye" (64). I have come to believe that it is only by opening our heart that we can truly find our bliss, and ultimately experience apotheosis.

For millennia, sages have taught that the best way to open our heart is through meditation. My favorite way to meditate is by just walking in beautiful and serene natural places away from the noise and business of the city. Spend time in the woods or on a quiet beach or lakeshore, just sitting or walking and truly paying attention to what is around you. Quiet your mind and just listen, and experience the natural world though your senses. I recommend you check out the concept of Japanese Shinrin-yoku, or forest bathing. I have experienced this as a powerful form of non-traditional meditation and enjoyed it so much that I offered a retreat called "Into the Woods" using this method along with qigong exercises. On the retreat, as I was looking around, I noticed an oak leaf hanging from a branch just at my eye level. The late morning sun shone through it from behind, causing it to be translucent and illuminating it as if it was shining from within. As I looked at it in detail, I noticed that the veins of the leaf shared a similar design with the tree to which it was attached. It had a large vein, or trunk, branching off into smaller veins at angles, and yet smaller veins branching from each of them. After examining this pattern on the leaf for a while I looked over at the river. It struck me that the river had basically the same design as the leaf and the tree. Beginning at its source, the river has a main branch and divides into smaller streams and creeks. I noticed that my own body has a trunk which also branches off into arms and legs and a head which further branch into fingers, toes, and hair. In Chinese Medicine, the energy channels have the same basic design: larger meridians branching off into smaller ones. I recalled the words of Jesus, "I am the vine; you are the branches" (John 15:5). I began to feel a deep tingling sensation and joy welling up inside as these realizations of connection continued to develop. I remembered reading that the molecular structure of hemoglobin in our blood and of chlorophyl in plants are nearly identical. The main difference is that hemoglobin is red because of one iron atom at its core and chlorophyl is green because of one magnesium atom at its core. Again, an amazing oneness. It struck me that if Jesus is the vine and we are the branches, then the Divine Energy that flowed through Jesus also flows through and nourishes us and I could feel, for a brief time, this divine energy flowing through me and tears welled up in my eyes. We cannot make our heart open by willpower. We can only prepare ourselves and be open when our inner wisdom or the Divine decides we are ready.

As strange as it may seem, perhaps the most powerful way to open our heart is through *amor fati*, a Latin translation of the Greek Stoic philosophy of loving one's fate. Amor fati is the realization that everything that happens in life, including our suffering and loss, is good. It is a mindset in which we make the best out of anything and everything that happens. Master Hong was once asked by a student if he believed in fate. He responded that he did. Our fate, he said, is created by three things: The original qi we inherit from our ancestors, or what we now call our DNA; the choices we make every moment of our life; and good and bad luck—things that just happen by chance.

We often judge our fate as either good or bad, but it is just what it is. To resist what is beyond our control condemns us to suffering. We certainly have some influence on our fate by the choices we make, but cannot completely control it. Opening our heart is necessary to learn to love one's fate. A counselee once said to me that they had discovered that life was not a problem to be solved, but a mystery to be lived. That is amor fati. The application of accepting, blending, and redirecting can be very helpful in living a life of amor fati. Accept what has happened as just fate; blending with it by trying to understand it as best you can and loving it. Finally redirect your path by making choices that will move you along a better path if the fates allow. The "one thing" involves discovering how we are called to work within our fate and still become a whole person.

## Chapter Twelve: One Thing

This brings us back to the Holy Grail legend. The young knight Percival, during his training, is told that a knight does not ask unnecessary questions. As a result, while in the mystical Grail Castle, he fails to ask the compassionate question that would heal the king and the land. This question varies depending on the version of the story. The questions are: What ails thee? Why do you suffer so? Whom does the Grail serve? Failing to ask the question, Percival wakes in the morning to find the castle empty and it disappears as he rides away. He has failed in his quest. Soon Percival meets a bereaved woman who he discovers is his cousin. She tells him why the Grail Castle disappeared and reveals to him the question he should have asked the Fisher King. Knowledge of the question, however is not enough. Percival must first open his heart and be able to ask the question with compassion and love. He spends several years trying to find the Grail Castle again. On the quest, he has many adventures and learns life lessons that open his heart. When he finally finds the Grail Castle again, he listens to his heart, asks the Fisher King the question, and the king and the land are healed. Percival has attained apotheosis. He is taught the secrets of the Grail, marries his true love, and becomes the Grail King himself.

Like all myths, the value of the Grail Legend is in discovering how it applies to our own life. The goal of our personal hero's journey must involve not only healing the wounds of the community but healing the wounded king (the Self) who dwells in the Castle of our Heart. Jung once wrote, "That I feed the hungry, forgive an insult, and love my enemy, these are great virtues. But what if I should discover that the poorest of the beggars and the most impudent of offenders are all within me; and that I stand in need of the alms of my own kindness, that I, myself, am the enemy who must be loved, what then?" (CW 11) Perhaps, like Sir Percival, when faced with our inner wounds, we must ask ourselves why we suffer so and whom the Grail in our heart serves. If on our hero's journey we discover this, we are close to finding our own "one thing." Joseph Campbell said, "We're not on our journey to save the world but to save ourselves. But in doing that you save the world," (183). Once we have found our Grail and healed our own inner wounds, we can live in the liminal place between the physical world and the trans-physical or spiritual realities. If we reach apotheosis, we are comfortable in both worlds. We are comfortable with other cultures, races, and spiritualities. We can follow logical conclusions, and listen to unconscious guidance. We balance right and left brain, masculine and feminine energies, and mind and heart. We can finally, as Craig Chalquist says, "see life as truly magical again."

# Postscript

In his poem, *Little Gidding*, T.S. Eliot wrote, "With the drawing of this love and the voice of this calling, we shall not cease from exploration. And the end of all our exploring will be to arrive where we started and know the place for the first time" (Four Quartets, Little Gidding, p. 49). My hero's journey began with my little girl's fever and my experience of warm energy flowing into her. This triggering event was my Call to Adventure on the quest to understand how this could have happened. While I tried to convince myself that this was primarily a scientific search, what I really wanted, perhaps unconsciously at the time, was to discover the secret of harnessing this healing magic at will. Over the course of my journey, as I began to work with people who were experiencing chronic pain and cancer, I wanted to be able to make their pain go away permanently. I wanted to make the cancer in their body disappear and never return. My stumbling block, for a very long time, was that the focus of my search was actually on me. Joseph Campbell, who through his writings and interviews had become a mentor to me, recognized this pitfall. He cautioned that questing was not an ego trip, but rather an adventure to discover our gift to the world. A hero, Campbell advised, is someone who has given their life to something bigger than themselves.

I came to realize along my journey that when I informed others, I did not want to work with people who were dying, it was not death that I was trying to avoid. My near-death experience did away with any fear of death itself. What I was really trying to avoid was seeing people in great suffering. This was in contrast to my perceived calling to work with the brokenhearted.

I had to face my fear and instead of avoiding suffering in others, I had to move toward their suffering. I had a dream that addressed this paradox in my calling to be a healer. In my dream I am on a large ferry boat. I am trying to get somewhere, but I don't know where. Someone says, "It's just a wild goose chase." Another person says in a frightened voice that there is a bear on the ship. Everyone is afraid. I go to find the bear and someone else says, "It just a wild goose chase." I find the bear in a storage room. It has a wound on its paw that looks raw and bloody. I take a container of salve from my pocket and slowly enter the room talking calmly to the bear. I am very frightened. I continue talking gently telling the bear that I am going to help. The bear growls and I am even more afraid. It finally allows me to approach and I put salve on its paw. When I am finished, the bear leaves the room, jumps into the water and swims away. Someone says, "It's just a wild goose chase." This was a powerfully symbolic dream for me. I am frightened of the suffering bear, but am drawn to it to provide some relief for its suffering. The idiom, "It's a wild goose chase," usually refers to a hopeless and foolhardy pursuit of something unreachable. Paradoxically, the Wild Goose, in Celtic Christianity, is an image of the Holy Spirit. The meaning I drew from this paradoxical phrase in my dream is that I am called by the Holy Spirit to be a healer using methods that other professionals may view as something foolish.

I still do not know how to make what happened with my daughter come about whenever I so desire. Perhaps my fatherly love for my daughter somehow tapped into Divine Love which passed through my open heart and into her. Psychiatrist Karl Menninger pondered on this idea. He believed that love cures people, both the giver and the receiver. I have come to accept the wisdom of the character, Old Lodge Skins, who said, in the 1970 film *Little Big Man*, "Well, sometimes the magic works and sometimes it doesn't." And while I never found a definitive answer to my original question as I had hoped, I have learned many things along my journey. I have learned the importance of loving my fate (*amor fati*). In loving my fate, I have found that my "one thing" is bringing peace to the brokenhearted and the suffering who find their way to me. I am here to help relieve their pain, when, and to the degree to which I am able, and to be a mentor and companion to them on their own hero's journey, even when that journey is nearing their death, and then, to function as a midwife helping their soul to be reborn into the afterworld.

I have also learned that when we discover our "one thing," our bliss, help will come through dreams, mentors, and synchronicity. Joseph Campbell discovered this too. While he proclaimed that he was not superstitious, he believed in what he characterized as spiritual magic. He once said that, "If one follows what I call one's bliss, the thing that really gets you deep in your gut and that you feel is your life, doors will open up. They do! They have in my life and they have in many lives that I know of," (An Open Life with Michael Tom. p.24). This has certainly been true for me.

I have come to think that the stage of apotheosis on the hero's journey is not a permanent state of being, except perhaps for a few living saints, bodhisattvas, and tzadikim, I have read about. But we can all experience this state of union through meditation, prayer, in places of natural beauty, and in times of great love and intimacy with others.

I have come to think that there is no meaning in suffering in itself, but that we can find meaning even in the midst of our suffering. Viktor Frankl described this in his book, *Man's Search for Meaning*. He wrote:

> We who lived in concentration camps can remember the men who walked through the huts comforting others, giving away their last piece of bread. They may have been few in number, but they offer sufficient proof that everything can be taken from a man but one thing; the last of the human freedoms—to choose one's attitude in any given set of circumstances, to choose one's own way . . . It is this spiritual

freedom—which cannot be taken away—that makes life meaningful and purposeful (27).

The hero's journey is at the heart of almost all the great stories in film and literature that survive the test of time. Somewhere between the religious fundamentalists and the scientific fundamentalists, there are untold numbers of seekers wandering along on their own hero's journey. You dear reader are one of them. Their hero's journey can be metaphorical or a real-life adventure. Some journeys are embarked upon by choice and some are chosen by destiny or perhaps Divine prompting. Everyone on their journey will be confronted with challenges and failures that are integral to revealing one's calling and purpose. Joseph Campbell assures us that we are not alone on our journey. All of the heroes of the past have gone before us. So too, every rambler will meet mentors and fellow travelers who will help them find their way when they feel lost and help them to overcome obstacles. I am confident that as each traveler continues on their hero's journey, it will be well worth the difficulties and challenges.

Finally, I have learned one more thing. In the movie, *The Best Exotic Marigold Hotel*, the young hero, Sonny explains, "There is a saying in India: Everything will be all right in the end. If it is not all right, then it is not yet the end." I, God willing, still have many years to walk the Way, and while everything is not perfectly all right with my aging body, the earth, or her people and creatures, I have faith that everything will be all right in the end, or it is not yet the end. Maybe, someday you will find what you are looking for, or maybe you won't. But maybe, just maybe, you will find something much greater than that. Meanwhile, I'll just keep walking and pondering on the Way and I hope that this book will somehow help you on your journey.

# Bibliography

Anapol, Deborah. *What Is Love and What it Isn't*. Psychology Today Online. Nov 25, 2011.

Aziz, Robert. C. G. *Jung's Psychology of Religion and Synchronicity*, Albany: State University of New York Press, 1990.

Balis, Jordan. *Common Ground: An Introduction to Eastern Christianity for the American Christian*. Minneapolis: Light & Life Publishing, 1991.

Benor, Daniel J. *Spiritual Healing and Psychotherapy*. The Therapist (UK) Winter 1994. Web. 22 Oct. 2017.

Bettelheim, Bruno. *The Uses of Enchantment: The Meaning and Importance of Fairy Tales*. Alfred A. Knott, 1976.

Campbell, Joseph, *The Hero with a Thousand Faces*. Princeton: Princeton University Press, 1972.

Campbell, Joseph. *Historical Atlas of World Mythology*. New York. Harper and Row, 1988.

Campbell, Joseph, ed. *The Portable Jung*. New York: Penguin Books, 1971.

Capra, Fritjof. *The Tao of Physics: An Exploration of the Parallels Between Modern Physics and Eastern Mysticism*, Boston: Shambhala Press, 1975.

Chalquist, Craig. *Why I seldom teach The Hero's Journey Anymore and What I Teach Instead*. The Huffington Post Online, 2017.

Chittister, Joan. *In Search of Belief.* Ligouri: Ligouri/Triumph, 1999.

Chuang Tsu. Basic Writings. Translated by Burton Watson. New York: Columbia University Press, 1996.

Cohen, Kenneth S. *The Way of Qigong: The Art and Science of Chinese Energy Healing.* New York: Ballantine Books. 1997.

Combs, Alan and Mark Holland. *Synchronicity: through the eyes of science, myth, and the trickster.* New York: Marlowe and Company, 1996.

Common English Bible. Grand Rapids: Abingdon Press, 2011.

Complete Jewish Bible. Clarksville: Jewish New Testament Publications, 1998.

Coniaris, Anthony M. *Theosis: Achieving Your Potential in Christ.* Minneapolis: Light & Life Publishing, 1993.

Cortright, Brant. *Psychotherapy and Spirit: Theory and Practice in Transpersonal Psychotherapy.* Albany: State University of New York Press, 1997.

Cousineau, Phil. *Coincidence or Destiny.* York Beach: Conari Press, 1997.

Eliot, T.S. *Four Quartets 4: Little Gidding.* Houghton Mifflin Harcourt. 1943.

Emerson, Ralph Waldo. Religion. *The Present Age Lecture 7.* Boston, Jan 1840.

Epperly, Bruce G. *God's Touch: Faith, Wholeness, and the Healing Miracles of Jesus.* Louisville: Westminster John Knox Press. 2001.

*Process Theology and the Healing Adventure: Reflections on Spirituality and Medicine.* Handbook of Process Theology. Ed. McDaniel, Jay and Donna Bowman, Atlanta: Chalice Press, 2006.

## Bibliography

Evans, Donald. *A Shamanic Christian Approach in Psychotherapy."
ranspersonal Psychotherapy. Second Edition.* Ed. Seymour Boorstein.
New York: State University of New York Press. 1996.

Feinstein, David, Eden, Donna, Craig, Gary. *The Promise of Energy Psychology.*
New York: Jeremy P. Tarcher, 2005.

Ferrauiola, Rex. *Synchronicity as the Work of the Holy Spirit.* Tenafly:
Self Published, 2011.

Forti, Kathy J. *Healing through Dream Incubation.* Trinfinity & Beyond.
Web. Feb. 2018.

Frankel, Estelle. *Sacred Therapy; Jewish Spiritual Teachings on emotional Healing
and Inner Wholeness.* Shambhala Publications, 2003.

Frankl, Viktor. *Man's Search for Meaning.* Beacon Press, 2006.

Frazer, James George. *The Golden Bough: A Study in Magic and Religion.*
The MacMillan Company, 1921.

Gamvas, Nicholas V. The *Psychology of Confession and the Orthodox Church.*
Minneapolis: Light and Light Publishing, 18989.

Gates, Thomas. *Reclaiming the Transcendent: God in Process.* Wallingford:
Pendle Hill Publications, 2013.

Geffin, Jeremy. *The Journey Through Cancer: Healing and Transforming
he Whole Person.* Three Rivers Press, 2006.

Glasser, William. *Reality Therapy.* Harper Collins, 1975.

*Gospel According to Thomas.* Scholars Version. Web. 16 Nov. 2017.

Hammerschlag, Carl A. *The Dancing Healers: A Doctor's Journey of Healing with Native Americans.* Harper and Row, 1988.

Hollis, James. *The Eden Project: In Search of the Magical Other.* Toronto: Inner City Books, 1998.

Hudson, Joyce Rockwood. *Natural Spirituality: Recovering the Wisdom Tradition in Christianity.* Danielsville: JRH Publications, 1998.

Jaffe, Lawrence W. *Liberating the Heart: Spirituality and Jungian Psychology.* Toronto: Inner City Books, 1990.

Johanson, Greg. Kurtz, Ron. *Grace Unfolding: Psychotherapy in the Spirit of the Tao-te-ching.* New York: Random House, 1991.

Jung, C. G. *Memories, Dreams, Reflections.* New York: Random House, 1963.

*On the Nature of the Psyche: Collected Works, 8.* Princeton: Princeton University Press, 1972.

*On Synchronicity: Collected Works, 8,* Princeton: Princeton University Press, 1972.

*Psychology and Alchemy (Collected Works of C.G. Jung Vol.12)* Princeton University Press, 1980.

*The Red Book: A Reader's Edition.* Ed. Sonu Shamdasani. NewYork: W. W. Norton & Company, 2009. Print.

*Jung on Mythology.* Ed. Robert A. Segal. New Jersey. Princeton University Press, 1998.

Jung, Emma and Marie-Loiuse von Franz. *The Grail Legend.* Princeton University Press, 1970.

## Bibliography

Kelsey, Morton T. *Self-Healing Practices for Bodymind Health*. New York: Crossroads Publishing, 1982.

Lacska, Yanchy, Lam, Paul. *Enrich Your Practice Through Imagery*. Taijiquan Journal, Summer 2001.

Lao Tsu, Translated by J. H. McDonald, *Tao Te Ching: An insightful and modern translation*. Penguin Publishing Group, 1992.

Layton, Jennifer. *The Taoist Mystical Experience: Analysis of the Numinous and Mystical Aspects*.

Lewis, C.S. *The Lion, the Witch, and the Wardrobe*. New York: Harper Collins, 1978.

Liu, Hong, with Paul Perry. *Mastering Miracles: The Healing Art of Qigong*. New York: Warner Books, 1997.

Main, Roderick. *Jung on Synchronicity and the Paranormal*. London: Routledge, 1997.

Maslow, Abraham. *The Farther Reaches of Human Nature*. Penguin Books, 1976.

May, Gerald G. *Care of Mind Care of Spirit*. New York: Harper Collins, 1992.

*The Dark Night of the Soul: A Psychiatrist Explores the Connection Between Darkness and Spiritual Growth*. New York: 2004.

*A Pilgrimage of Healing: Personal Thoughts of a Transpersonal Psychotherapist*. Ed. Seymour Boorstein, Second Edition. Albany: State University of York Press, 1996.

Mayer, Michael. *Energy Psychology: Self-Healing Practices for Bodymind Health*. Berkeley: North Atlantic Books, 2009.

McNamara, William. *Psychology and the Christian Mystical Tradition.* Transpersonal Psychologies. Ed. Charles T. Tart. New York: Harper and Row, 1975.

Mill, Jon. "Jung's Metaphysics." *International Journal of Jungian Studies.* 2012. Web. 3 May 2018.

Miller, Emmett E. *Deep Healing: The Essence of Mind/Body Medicine.* Carlsbad: Hay House, 1997.

Minick, Michael. *The Wisdom of Kung Fu.* New York: William Morrow & Co, 1974.

Montemayor, Carlos. *Minding Time: A Philosophical and Theoretical Approach to the Psychology of Time.* Brill, 2013.

Moser, Fanny. Spuk. *Ein Rätsel der Menschheit.* Olten: Walter, 1977 (1950).

Moyers, Bill, Campbell, Joseph, *The Power of Myth.* PBS series, 1988.

Newell, J. Philip, *Listening for The Heartbeat of God: A Celtic Spirituality*, Mahwah, Paulist Press, 1997.

Newell, J. Philip, *Christ of the Celts: The Healing of Creation*, San Francisco, Jossey-Bass, 2008.

Ni, Preston C. *How to Remember and Learn from Your Dreams*, Psychology Today, February 15, 2022. Online.

*Oxford New Revised Standard Version Bible*, New York, Oxford University Press, 1990.

Pargament, Kenneth I. *Spiritually Integrated Psychotherapy: Understanding and Addressing the Sacred.* New York: The Guilford Press, 2007.

# BIBLIOGRAPHY

Pascal, Blaise, *Pensées* published by Penguin Books, London: 1995

Poluboyarinova, Alexandra. *The Spiritual Heart: God's Channel: An Interview with Alexander Mumrikov.* Inward Path Magazine. Issue 92, Georgetown: Inward Path Publishers, 1993.

Sanderson, Ruth, *The Enchanted Wood.* Little, Brown and Company, 1991.

Sanford, Agnes. *The Healing Light.* Plainfield: Logos International. 1972.

Sanford, John A. *Healing and Wholeness*, New York: Paulist Press. 1977.

Slade, Andrew. *Guide to the Superior Hiking Trail.* Toledo: Discover Books, 1993

*Star Wars.* George Lucas. 20th Century Fox, 1977.

*Star Wars: The Empire Strikes Back.* George Lucas. 20th Century Fox, 1980.

*Star Wars: The Last Jedi.* J. J. Abrams. Disney Films, 2017.

Stein, Murray, *Jung's Map of the Soul: An Introduction.* Open Court Press, 1998.

Sweet, Victoria, *Slow Medicine The Way To Healing.* Silverhead Books, 2017.

Tarnas, Richard. *Cosmos and Psyche: Intimations of a New World View*, April 24, 2007

Tolkien, J.R.R. *The Fellowship of the Ring.* Ballantine Books, 1974.

Turner, Kelly A. *Radical Remission: Surviving Cancer Against All Odds.* New York: Harper Collins, 2014.

Ueshiba, Morihei. *The Art of Peace.* Shambhala Publications, 2002.

Weatherhead Leslie D. *Psychology, Religion and Healing*. Nashville: Abingdon—Cokesbury Press. 1975.

Whitman, Walt. *Leaves of Grass*. New York: Simon Schuster, 2006.

Wilhelm, Richard (With a Commentary by C.G. Jung). *The Secret of the Golden Flower*. Orlando: Harcourt Brace Jovanovic, 1962.

Wilhelm, Richard, Baynes, C. F. *The I Ching or Book of Changes*. Princeton: Princeton University Press, 1977.

# *Acknowledgments*

Writing a book about my own life was a much more challenging and labyrinthian task than I would have ever imagined. I placed a copy of the following quote by Anne Lamott above my computer, to remind me to keep writing during the numerous times I lost my confidence. "I don't think you have time to waste not writing because you are afraid you won't be good at it" (Bird by Bird).

Several of the individuals who influenced my story were introduced in the pages of the book itself. I have included this page to acknowledge those, who while not appearing in any detail in the stories presented in this memoir, have influenced my life, and made it possible to arrive at the point in my journey where I could write this book.

First and foremost are my children, Deborah, Christine, John, and my stepson Andrew. All of them have taught me how to love better, and to be a helpful guide on their own journeys in life. They have made me very proud. Each of them works in a helping profession: Debbie is a school counselor, Chrissie is a registered nurse and Salvation Army officer, John is a peace officer, and Andrew is completing his education to be a licensed professional counselor. In addition, they have all made me a gloating grandfather.

I am also appreciative of the teachers I did not mention in my story, Dr. Ma Xuzhou who taught me qigong skills that have become an important part of both my daily life and my counseling practice, and my tai chi teacher and friend, Dr. Paul Lam, whose brilliant teaching method is the one I always use when teaching qigong exercises to groups or individuals. I also have heartfelt gratitude for all the college professors and seminary teachers who broadened and challenged my thinking. I also wish to express my appreciation for Sister Marian Louwagie, may her soul rest in peace, who allowed me to combine chaplaincy, psychology, and qigong healing in a hospital setting.

My thanks and respect to all those who taught the seminars and classes at the Minnesota Jung Association, for helping me to acquire, and in turn, incorporate the ideas of C.G. Jung and other depth psychologists into my work. And while they are long deceased, I must acknowledge Joseph Campbell and Carl Jung for their influence on my thinking, teaching, and counseling.

Finally, I am full of gratitude for all my students and counselees who formed the real crucible in which I learned how to put into practice my integrative transpersonal approach to counseling.

# About the Author

Y.R. Lacska, PhD has always been a seeker. His search has led him on a career path that included being a teacher, psychotherapist, college professor, emergency management coordinator, and hospital chaplain. Since childhood, he has been an avid practitioner of the Asian martial arts, qigong, tai chi, and the Taoist philosophy at their core. He continues his work as a pastoral counselor and offers workshops and retreats combining his knowledge of psychology with the wisdom of the world's spiritual traditions and qigong. To learn more about the author visit his website revyanchylacska.com

www.ingramcontent.com/pod-product-compliance
Lightning Source LLC
LaVergne TN
LVHW041704060526
838201LV00043B/569